React Components

Explore the power of React components
for cutting-edge web development

Christopher Pitt

PUBLISHING

BIRMINGHAM - MUMBAI

React Components

First published: April 2016

Production reference: 1180416

Published by Packt Publishing Ltd.
Livery Place
35 Livery Street
Birmingham B3 2PB, UK.

ISBN 978-1-78588-928-8

www.packtpub.com

Credits

Author
Christopher Pitt

Reviewer
Konstantin Tarkus

Commissioning Editor
Wilson D'souza

Acquisition Editor
Aaron Lazar

Content Development Editor
Parshva Sheth

Technical Editor
Madhunikita Sunil Chindarkar

Copy Editor
Pranjali Chury

Project Coordinator
Nikhil Nair

Proofreader
Safis Editing

Indexer
Tejal Daruwale Soni

Production Coordinator
Manu Joseph

Cover Work
Manu Joseph

About the Author

Christopher Pitt is a principal developer for SilverStripe in Wellington, New Zealand. He usually works on open source software, though sometimes you'll find him building compilers and robots.

I'd like to thank SilverStripe for supporting open source, in general, and for my growth as a developer, in particular. Many folks have helped me through the process of writing this book, especially the open source and platform teams at SilverStripe. Thanks to everyone who answered a question, gave me writing advice, and shared their excitement about React with me. They are the authors of this book as much as I am.

I'd also like to thank my family, especially my patient and loving wife.

About the Reviewer

Konstantin Tarkus is a long-time software developer and the founder and CTO of Kriasoft—a software development company specializing in building web and cloud applications. He is the author of *React Starter Kit*—a popular open source boilerplate project for building isomorphic web applications with Node.js and React, which is used by many tech start-ups around the globe. You can reach out to him on Twitter at `@koistya`.

www.PacktPub.com

eBooks, discount offers, and more

Did you know that Packt offers eBook versions of every book published, with PDF and ePub files available? You can upgrade to the eBook version at www.PacktPub.com and as a print book customer, you are entitled to a discount on the eBook copy. Get in touch with us at customercare@packtpub.com for more details.

At www.PacktPub.com, you can also read a collection of free technical articles, sign up for a range of free newsletters and receive exclusive discounts and offers on Packt books and eBooks.

https://www2.packtpub.com/books/subscription/packtlib

Do you need instant solutions to your IT questions? PacktLib is Packt's online digital book library. Here, you can search, access, and read Packt's entire library of books.

Why subscribe?

- Fully searchable across every book published by Packt
- Copy and paste, print, and bookmark content
- On demand and accessible via a web browser

Table of Contents

Preface

React is a fascinating new take on traditional frontend development. It has taken the JavaScript community by storm and has inspired sweeping changes in a number of existing JavaScript application frameworks and architectures.

Unfortunately, there still aren't many examples of great architecture. Most tutorials and books focus on small components and examples, leaving the question of larger applications and component hierarchies unanswered. That is what this book seeks to change.

What this book covers

Chapter 1, Thinking in Components, looks at the need to think of entire interfaces as a composition of small components and how to build them using modern ES6 JavaScript.

Chapter 2, Working with Properties and State, takes a comprehensive look at many aspects of property and state management, sharing a few more ES6 tricks along the way.

Chapter 3, Saving and Communicating Data, looks at reactive programming using event emitters and unidirectional flow of data.

Chapter 4, Styling and Animating Components, takes a look at how components can be styled and animated both inline and using stylesheets.

Chapter 5, Going Material!, explores material design and applies what you learn to our set of components.

Chapter 6, Changing Views, looks at ways of transitioning between different views with routing and animation.

Chapter 7, Rendering on the Server, takes a look at the process of rendering components through nodes and some ways of structuring server-side application code.

Chapter 8, React Design Patterns, explores different architectures such as Flux and Redux.

Chapter 9, Thinking of Plugins, looks at how to build components with dependency injection and extension points.

Chapter 10, Testing Components, explores various ways of ensuring that components are error-free and that changes to parts of an application don't have cascading effects on other parts.

What you need for this book

The following hardware is recommended for maximum enjoyment:

- Any modern computer with Linux, Mac OS, or Windows.

All software mentioned in this book are free of charge and can be downloaded from the Internet.

Who this book is for

This book is ideal for developers who are familiar with the basics of React and are looking for a guide to build a wide range of components as well as develop component-driven UIs.

Conventions

In this book, you will find a number of text styles that distinguish between different kinds of information. Here are some examples of these styles and an explanation of their meaning.

Code words in text, database table names, folder names, filenames, file extensions, pathnames, dummy URLs, user input, and Twitter handles are shown as follows: "We need to register a default set of tasks, which we set to browserify and uglify."

A block of code is set as follows:

```
"scripts": {
    "bundle": "browserify -t babelify main.js -o main.dist.js",
    "minify": "..."
}
```

When we wish to draw your attention to a particular part of a code block, the relevant lines or items are set in bold:

```
render() {
    if (this.state.isEditing) {
        return <PageEditor {...this.props} />;
    }

    return <PageView {...this.props} />;
}
```

Any command-line input or output is written as follows:

```
$ npm install --save-dev grunt
$ npm install --save-dev grunt-browserify
$ npm install --save-dev grunt-contrib-uglify
$ npm install --save-dev grunt-contrib-watch
```

New terms and **important words** are shown in bold. Words that you see on the screen, for example, in menus or dialog boxes, appear in the text like this: "To get the most out of JSBin, be sure to set the **JavaScript** dropdown to **ES6/Babel** and include the ReactJS scripts from *CDNJS*."

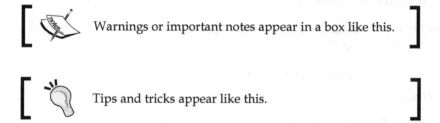

Warnings or important notes appear in a box like this.

Tips and tricks appear like this.

Reader feedback

Feedback from our readers is always welcome. Let us know what you think about this book—what you liked or disliked. Reader feedback is important for us as it helps us develop titles that you will really get the most out of.

To send us general feedback, simply e-mail feedback@packtpub.com, and mention the book's title in the subject of your message.

If there is a topic that you have expertise in and you are interested in either writing or contributing to a book, see our author guide at www.packtpub.com/authors.

Customer support

Now that you are the proud owner of a Packt book, we have a number of things to help you to get the most from your purchase.

Downloading the example code

You can download the example code files for this book from your account at `http://www.packtpub.com`. If you purchased this book elsewhere, you can visit `http://www.packtpub.com/support` and register to have the files e-mailed directly to you.

You can download the code files by following these steps:

1. Log in or register to our website using your e-mail address and password.
2. Hover the mouse pointer on the **SUPPORT** tab at the top.
3. Click on **Code Downloads & Errata**.
4. Enter the name of the book in the **Search** box.
5. Select the book for which you're looking to download the code files.
6. Choose from the drop-down menu where you purchased this book from.
7. Click on **Code Download**.

Once the file is downloaded, please make sure that you unzip or extract the folder using the latest version of:

- WinRAR / 7-Zip for Windows
- Zipeg / iZip / UnRarX for Mac
- 7-Zip / PeaZip for Linux

Errata

Although we have taken every care to ensure the accuracy of our content, mistakes do happen. If you find a mistake in one of our books—maybe a mistake in the text or the code—we would be grateful if you could report this to us. By doing so, you can save other readers from frustration and help us improve subsequent versions of this book. If you find any errata, please report them by visiting `http://www.packtpub.com/submit-errata`, selecting your book, clicking on the **Errata Submission Form** link, and entering the details of your errata. Once your errata are verified, your submission will be accepted and the errata will be uploaded to our website or added to any list of existing errata under the Errata section of that title.

To view the previously submitted errata, go to https://www.packtpub.com/books/content/support and enter the name of the book in the search field. The required information will appear under the **Errata** section.

Piracy

Piracy of copyrighted material on the Internet is an ongoing problem across all media. At Packt, we take the protection of our copyright and licenses very seriously. If you come across any illegal copies of our works in any form on the Internet, please provide us with the location address or website name immediately so that we can pursue a remedy.

Please contact us at copyright@packtpub.com with a link to the suspected pirated material.

We appreciate your help in protecting our authors and our ability to bring you valuable content.

Questions

If you have a problem with any aspect of this book, you can contact us at questions@packtpub.com, and we will do our best to address the problem.

1
Thinking in Components

React was the first interface library that got me thinking about component-based design. React promotes many good patterns and habits, but this one stands out for me. To understand why, we need to think about how React works under the hood. React is primarily a rendering engine. It was created (and is used) for generating user interfaces.

How interfaces used to work (and indeed still work apart from React) was that someone would come up with a design. That image file would then be split up into assets for each interactive part of the interface. A library such as jQuery would manage user interactions and connect different interface components, often with an assortment of plugins.

Individual interface components can be quite clean and complete individually. However, when they are combined, interactions between components and shared, mutable component state often make a messy codebase. One of the main reasons why React was created was to simplify the interactions between components, so they can remain clean and easy to understand.

Why components?

Component-based design is powerful, especially when we use immutable data and unidirectional data flow. It forces me to stop thinking about how different technologies or tools interact. It gets me thinking about the single most important function of each interface element.

When we start building an application, it's tempting to think of every piece as part of the whole. All interface elements blend into the same big picture, until it becomes so big that separating parts of it out seems impossible.

Imagine you had to build a space ship. What a huge task! You'd need some rocket boosters, a couple of wings, life support, and so on. Now consider how you would approach it if one of the constraints was that each moving part of the space ship would need to be individually tested.

Testing is the great divide between designing systems as a whole and designing systems as large collections of small pieces. Component-based design is fantastic because it makes sure that every part is testable.

Using modern JavaScript

React components are wonderfully encapsulated. Each component is a blueprint for what a focused bit of markup should look like at any moment. They're reusable and can change their behavior depending on the context provided. Does that remind you of another programming paradigm?

Let's talk about JavaScript. JavaScript has a prototypical inheritance model. That means different objects can have a common structure. The structure of one object can be derived from the structure of another.

It also means that changes to the original object are inherited in all derivative objects. Let me illustrate this with some code:

```javascript
var Page = function(content) {
    this.content = content;
};

Page.prototype.render = function() {
    return "<div>" + this.content + "</div>";
}

var Post = function(tags, content) {
    this.tags = tags;

    Page.call(this, content);
};

Post.prototype = new Page();

Post.prototype.render = function() {
    var page = Page.prototype.render.call(this);

    return "<ul>" + this.renderTags() + "</ul>" + page;
};
```

```
Post.prototype.renderTags = function() {
    return "<li>" + this.tags.join("</li></li>") + "</li>";
};

var page = new Page("Welcome to my site!");
var post = new Post(["news"], "A new product!");

Page.prototype.render = function() {
    return "<section>" + this.content + "</section>";
};
```

I begin by creating a function called `Page`, which requires a `content` parameter. A simple `render` method returns that content, wrapped in a `div` tag. This seems like a good starting point for a website.

Next, I decide to make a second type called `Post`. Objects of this type have tags, so I create a new initialization function to store them. I want `Post` to behave almost like a `Page` type, so I call the `Page` initialization function.

To inherit the `Page` methods in `Post`, I need to link their prototypes. I can then choose to override the `render` method and add new methods to the derived type. I can also change the `Page` type and these changes will be inherited by objects of the `Post` type. The connection happens because a prototype is a reference and not a copy.

Depending on the programming languages you grew up with, prototypical inheritance might be tricky at first. Many new developers learn (incorrectly) that object-oriented code means class-oriented code. Dynamic concepts such as prototypes are foreign to them. In the past, this led to a few libraries implementing "pretend" classes. They created patterns that would make code appear as if it was class-oriented.

Then, ES6 added the `class` keyword. It's a formalization of the pattern I just showed you. It's a syntactic shortcut to prototypical inheritance.

We could reduce the previous code to:

```
class Page {
    constructor(content) {
        this.content = content;
    }

    render() {
        return "<div>" + this.content + "</div>";
    }
}
```

```
class Post extends Page {
    constructor(tags, content) {
        super(content);
        this.tags = tags;
    }

    render() {
        var page = super.render();

        return "<ul>" + this.renderTags() + "</ul>" + page;
    }

    renderTags() {
        return "<li>" + this.tags.join("</li></li>") + "</li>";
    }
}

var page = new Page("Welcome to my site!");
var post = new Post(["news"], "A new product!");
```

 If you're trying to run this using Node (preferably a version greater than 4.1), you may need to add use `strict` at the top of the file.

Notice how much clearer things are? If you want to use classes, then this syntactic shortcut is brilliant!

Let's look at a typical ES5-compatible React component:

```
var Page = React.createClass({
    render: function() {
        return <div>{this.props.content}</div>;
    }
});

var Post = React.createClass({
    render: function() {
        var page = <Page content={this.props.content} />
        var tags = this.renderTags();

        return <div><ul>{tags}</ul>{page}</div>;
    },
    renderTags: function() {
        return this.props.tags.map(function(tag, i) {
```

```
        return <li key={i}>{tag}</li>;
    });
}
});

ReactDOM.render(
    <Post tags={["news"]} content="A new product!" />,
    document.querySelector(".react")
);
```

You've probably seen this kind of code before. It's called JSX and it's a JavaScript superset language. The idea is that the markup and the supporting logic are created and stored together.

 React components must return a single React node, which is why we wrap the tags and page elements in a div element. If you are using React in the browser, you also need to render your components to an existing DOM node (like I've just rendered the post to .react).

We'll get into some of the specifics in later chapters, but this is doing pretty much the same thing as before. We create a base component called Page. It renders a property instead of a constructor parameter.

The Post component composes the Page component. This style of React code doesn't support component inheritance. For that, we need ES6 code:

```
class Page extends React.Component {
    render() {
        return <div>{this.props.content}</div>;
    }
}

class Post extends Page {
    render() {
        var page = super.render();
        var tags = this.renderTags();

        return <div><ul>{tags}</ul>{page}</div>;
    }

    renderTags() {
        return this.props.tags.map(function(tag, i) {
            return <li key={i}>{tag}</li>;
        });
    }
}
```

We could still compose Page within Post, but that's not the only option with ES6. This code resembles the non-React version we saw earlier.

In upcoming chapters, we'll learn many useful features of ES6 that'll allow us to create modern, expressive React components.

 If you want to look ahead a little, check out http://babeljs.io/ docs/learn-es2015. It's a great place to learn the main features of ES6!

Babel is the cross-compilation tool we'll use to turn ES6 code into ES5 code:

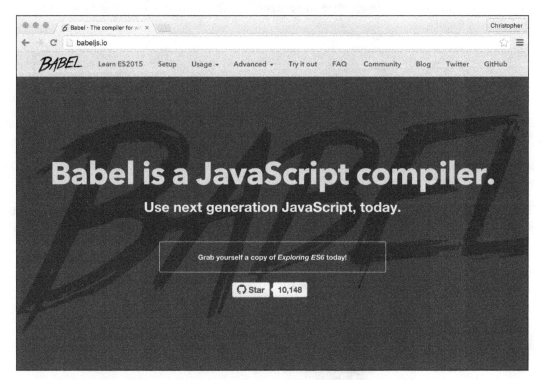

Compiling modern JavaScript

It's time for us to look at how to compile ES6 and JSX code into formats that most browsers can read. Create a folder for your React components and run the following commands inside it:

```
$ npm init
$ npm install --save browserify babelify
$ npm install --save react react-dom
```

The first command will kick off a series of questions, most of which should have reasonable defaults. The second command will download a builder and a cross-compiler for your ES6 code. Place the following component in a file called `page.js`:

```
import React from "react";

export default class Page extends React.Component {
    render() {
        return <div>{this.props.content}</div>;
    }
}
```

There are a couple of important differences between this and the previous `Page` component. We import the main `React` object from within the `node_modules` folder. We also export the class definition so that importing this file immediately references this class. It's a good idea to limit each file to a single class. It's also a good idea to make each file define types or use them. We use this class in `main.js`:

```
import React from "react";
import ReactDOM from "react-dom";
import Page from "./page";

ReactDOM.render(
    <Page content="Welcome to my site!" />,
    document.querySelector(".react")
);
```

This code imports `React` and `ReactDOM` from within the `node_modules` folder, so we can render the `Page` class. Here we're referencing an element in the DOM again. We can use this JavaScript within an HTML page:

```
<!doctype html>
<html lang="en">
    <body>
        <div class="react"></div>
    </body>
    <script src="main.dist.js"></script>
</html>
```

The final step is to compile the ES6/JSX code in `main.js` to ES5-compatible code in `main.dist.js`:

```
$ alias browserify=node_modules/.bin/browserify
$ browserify -t babelify main.js -o main.dist.js
```

The first command creates a shortcut to the `browserify` command in the `node_modules/.bin` folder. This is useful for repeated calls to `browserify`.

 If you want to keep that alias around, be sure to add it to your `~/.bashrc`, `~/.zshrc` or `~/.profile` file.

The second command starts a build. *Browserify* will combine all imported files into a single file, so they can be used in a browser.

We use the `babelify` transformer, so the ES6 code becomes ES5-compatible code. Babel supports JSX, so we don't need additional steps for that. We specify `main.js` as the file to transform and `main.dist.js` as the output file.

 If you want to compile React and ReactDOM into their own file, you can exclude them with the `-x` switch. Your command should be something like this:

```
browserify main.js -t babelify -x react -x react-dom
--outfile main.dist.js
```

Debugging in the browser

We can also use our code directly in the browser. There may be times when we want to see the effects of a change, without a build step. In such cases, we can try something like this:

```
$ npm install --save babel-core
```

```
$ npm install --save systemjs
```

These will give us access to a browser-based dependency manager and cross-compiler; that is, we can use unbundled source code in an example HTML file:

```
<!DOCTYPE html>
<html>
    <head>
        <script src="/node_modules/babel-core/browser.js"></script>
        <script src="/node_modules/systemjs/dist/system.js"></script>
    </head>
    <body>
        <div class="react"></div>
        <script>
            System.config({
                "transpiler": "babel",
                "map": {
                    "react": "/examples/react/react",
```

```
                    "react-dom": "/examples/react/react-dom",
                    "page": "/src/page"
                },
                "defaultJSExtensions": true
            });

            System.import("main");
        </script>
    </body>
</html>
```

This uses the same unprocessed `main.js` file as before, but we no longer need to rebuild it after each change to the source code. The `System` is a reference to the *SystemJS* library we just installed through NPM. It takes care of the import statements, loading those dependencies with Ajax requests.

You may notice the references to `react` and `react-dom`. We import these in `main.js`, but where do they come from? Browserify fetches them out of the `node_modules` folder. When we skip the Browserify step, we need to let SystemJS know where to find them.

The easiest place to find these files is at `https://facebook.github.io/react`. Click on the download button, extract the archive, and copy the `JS` files in the `build` folder to where they are referenced in the HTML page.

The ReactJS website is a great place to download ReactJS, and find documentation about how you can use it:

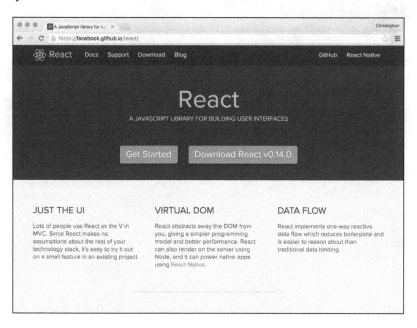

Managing common tasks

As our collection of React components grows, we'll need ways of bundling them all together. It would also be a good idea for us to minify the resulting JavaScript to reduce the time it takes to load them in a browser.

We can perform these kinds of tasks using scripts in `package.json`:

```
"scripts": {
    "bundle": "browserify -t babelify main.js -o main.dist.js",
    "minify": "..."
}
```

NPM scripts are fine for small, simple tasks. When the tasks get more complex, we'll start to see the drawbacks of using NPM scripts for this. There's no easy way to use variables in these scripts, so parameters are often repeated. The scripts are also a bit inflexible and frankly ugly.

There are a few tools that address these problems. We're going to use one of them, called **Grunt**, to create flexible, repeatable tasks.

The Grunt website has instructions for using Grunt and a list of popular plugins you can use to customize your workflow:

Grunt is a JavaScript task runner. There are three steps for using it:

1. First, we need to install the CLI tool. We'll use this to run different tasks.
2. Then, we need to install the libraries our tasks will use, via NPM.
3. Finally, we need to create a `gruntfile.js` file where we'll put our tasks.

We can install the CLI tool using the following command:

```
$ npm install -g grunt-cli
```

 The preceding command installs the Grunt CLI tool globally. If you don't want that, omit the -g flag. You'll need to alias/run it directly with `node_modules/.bin/grunt` from here on though.

We will need the following task libraries:

```
$ npm install --save-dev grunt
$ npm install --save-dev grunt-browserify
$ npm install --save-dev grunt-contrib-uglify
$ npm install --save-dev grunt-contrib-watch
```

The global CLI tool needs a local copy of `grunt`. In addition, we also want the glue libraries to run Browserify, Uglify, and a file watcher in Grunt. We configure them with something like this:

```
module.exports = function(grunt) {
    grunt.initConfig({
        "browserify": {
            "main.js": ["main.es5.js"],
            "options": {
                "transform": [
                    "babelify"
                ],
                "external": [
                    "react", "react-dom"
                ]
            }
        },
        "uglify": {
            "main.es5.js": ["main.dist.js"]
        },
        "watch": {
            "files": ["main.js"],
            "tasks": ["browserify", "uglify"]
```

```
        }
    });

    grunt.loadNpmTasks("grunt-browserify");
    grunt.loadNpmTasks("grunt-contrib-uglify");
    grunt.loadNpmTasks("grunt-contrib-watch");

    grunt.registerTask("default", ["browserify", "uglify"]);
};
```

We can configure each task in `gruntfile.js`. Here, we create a `browserify` task, defining the source and destination files. We include the `babelify` transformation to convert our ES6 classes into ES5-compatible code.

 I've added the `external` option so you can see how. If you don't need it, just delete it and your bundle file should then include the full React source code.

After the ES6 code is transformed, we can run *Uglify* to remove unnecessary whitespace. This reduces the size of the file, so browsers can download it quicker. We can target the file Browserify created and create a new minified file from it.

Finally, we create a `watch` task. This watches for changes to `main.js` and triggers the Browserify and Uglify tasks. We need to register a default set of tasks, which we set to `browserify` and `uglify`. This configuration enables the following commands:

```
$ grunt
$ grunt browserify
$ grunt uglify
$ grunt watch
```

There are other great tools like Grunt:

- `http://gulpjs.com`
- `https://webpack.github.io`

They work with similar configuration files, but the configuration is done through functional composition. The important thing to take from this is that there are tools we can use to automate tasks we would have run by hand. They make these repetitive tasks easy!

Testing in JSBin

If you're anything like me, you'll often just want a quick place to test some small component or ES6 code. Setting up these build chains or live browser environments takes time. There is a quicker way. It's called JSBin and you can find it at `https://jsbin.com`:

To get the most out of JSBin, be sure to set the **JavaScript** dropdown to **ES6/Babel** and include the ReactJS scripts from *CDNJS*. These are pre-built versions of ReactJS, so you can create React components (using ES6 features) straight from the browser.

Downloading the example code

You can download the example code files for this book from your account at `http://www.packtpub.com`. If you purchased this book elsewhere, you can visit `http://www.packtpub.com/support` and register to have the files e-mailed directly to you.

You can download the code files by following these steps:

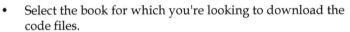

- Log in or register to our website using your e-mail address and password.
- Hover the mouse pointer on the SUPPORT tab at the top.
- Click on Code Downloads & Errata.
- Enter the name of the book in the Search box.
- Select the book for which you're looking to download the code files.
- Choose from the drop-down menu where you purchased this book from.
- Click on Code Download.

You can also download the code files by clicking on the Code Files button on the book's webpage at the Packt Publishing website. This page can be accessed by entering the book's name in the Search box. Please note that you need to be logged in to your Packt account.

Once the file is downloaded, please make sure that you unzip or extract the folder using the latest version of:

- WinRAR / 7-Zip for Windows
- Zipeg / iZip / UnRarX for Mac
- 7-Zip / PeaZip for Linux

Summary

In this chapter, we saw why component-based design is good. We saw what simple React components look like. We saw a few interesting differences between ES5 and ES6, and we also saw how those differences influence React components.

We also saw a few ways to make ES6 code work in an ES5-compatible way. We can write cutting-edge code that works on common browsers. We can even bundle that code into single, efficient files, or debug it live in a browser.

In the next chapter, we're going to look at some intricacies of state and properties. We'll begin by creating reusable React components to use in our example application.

2
Working with Properties and State

In the previous chapter, we set up our workflow. We worked out how to compile ReactJS and ES6 code through a build step, interpret it directly in our browser, and even run it using services such as JSBin. Now, we can begin creating components for our content management system.

In this chapter, we're going to start building our interface. We'll see interesting and effective ways to connect components. The important thing in this chapter is learning how to arrange components in complex hierarchies. We're going to nest several components and communicate between them and our data source, using a custom data backend.

Nesting components

Let's think about how we want to structure the components of our interface. Many content management systems feature lists of items—items that we store in and retrieve from a database. For example, let's imagine a system through which we can manage the pages of a website.

For such a system, we need an entry-point—something like `PageAdmin`, which connects our persistence layer to our interface:

```
import React from "react";

class PageAdmin extends React.Component {
    render() {
        return <ol>...page objects</ol>;
    }
```

```
    }

    export default PageAdmin;
```

We can also represent the persistence layer in the form of a backend class:

```
class Backend {
    getAll() {
        // ...returns an array of pages
    }

    update(id, property, value) {
        // ...updates a page
    }

    delete(id) {
        // ...deletes a page
    }
}
```

 Later, we'll look at ways of persisting this data.
For now, it's OK to just use static data in this class.

We could connect `PageAdmin` to this class by proving an instance of `Backend` as a property:

```
var backend = new Backend();

ReactDOM.render(
    <PageAdmin backend={backend} />,
    document.querySelector(".react")
);
```

Now, we can start using the `Backend` data in our `PageAdmin` component:

```
class PageAdmin extends React.Component {
    constructor(props) {
        super(props);

        this.state = {
            "pages": []
        };
    }
```

```
componentWillMount() {
    this.setState({
        "pages": this.props.backend.getAll()
    });
}

render() {
    return <ol>
        {this.state.pages.map(function(page) {
            return <li key={page.id}>a new page</li>
        })}
    </ol>;
}
}
```

 The truth is that we don't really need to define a default state, or store the page objects to the state. I've done so to demonstrate the idiomatic way of defining initial component state and overriding state when working with ES6-style components.

There's a lot going on here, so let's break it down bit-by-bit:

- We made a constructor. In the constructor, we defined the initial state of a component. We defined the state as an object with an empty pages array.

- React will call a few *magic* methods in the life cycle of a component. We used componentWillMount to get an array of pages, so we have something to render. We also passed this array of pages to the setState method. This exists to store state data and update the markup of a component at the same time. The this.state.pages method will now contain the array of pages from the backend.

- When we use curly braces inside markup, it acts like a dynamic value (just like with properties). We can use the Array.prototype.map method to return a new element for each page in the array of pages. This will return a new list of li components. React also expects components in a list to have a special key property, which it uses to identify them. React uses this to track which components it can remove, add, or change efficiently.

 The code references page.id. The pages returned by the backend should have the id, title, and body properties for these examples to work.

Let's concentrate on how to show each page through the content management system. The PageAdmin renders each page as a list item, so let's think about what we want to do inside each list item. I think it makes sense to have a non-interactive summary of each page. Think of a tabular view of all pages in a website:

- Home
- Products
- Terms of service
- Contact us

So there's one aspect to pages that is static: the view of the page title. Perhaps we can also include links to edit or delete each page.

We also want to be able to update each page. We're probably going to need some sort of form, with text inputs for each field we might want to update.

We can represent these two scenarios in a single component:

```
import React from "react";

class Page extends React.Component {
    constructor(props) {
        super(props);

        this.state = {
            "isEditing": false
        };
    }

    render() {
        if (this.state.isEditing) {
            return <PageEditor />;
        }

        return <PageView />;
    }
}

export default Page;
```

Now, we can switch between the different components, based on whether we're editing or not. Of course, we also need to define these new components:

```
import React from "react";

class PageEditor extends React.Component {
    render() {
        return <form>
            <input type="text" name="title" />
            <textarea name="body"></textarea>
            <button>back</button>
        </form>;
    }
}

export default PageEditor;
```

Note that we can define input elements in a way you might expect, if you've worked with HTML markup before. We'll revisit this component later, so don't worry about the details just yet.

The preview mode, for this component, is a little similar:

```
import React from "react";

class PageView extends React.Component {
    render() {
        return <div>
            {this.props.title}
            <button>edit</button>
            <button>delete</button>
        </div>;
    }
}

export default PageView;
```

This raises an interesting question. How can we efficiently transfer properties from one component to another? ES6 provides a great tool for this in the form of a language feature called the *spread* operator. First, we need to provide pages to page components in `PageAdmin`:

```
render() {
    return <ol>
        {this.state.pages.map(function(page) {
            return <li key={page.id}>
                <Page {...page} />
```

```
        </li>;
    })}
  </ol>;
}
```

We're replacing a `new page` with the `Page` component we created earlier. We use the spread operator to assign each object key as a component property. We can repeat this concept in `Page`:

```
render() {
    if (this.state.isEditing) {
        return <PageEditor {...this.props} />;
    }

    return <PageView {...this.props} />;
}
```

The `{...this.props}` expands the page object keys. The `page.id` becomes `this.props.id` inside the `PageEditor` and `PageView` components. This method is great for transferring many properties; we don't need to write out each one.

Shared component actions

So, how do we change from a `PageView` class to a `PageEditor` class? For that, we need to hook into browser events and fiddle with the state:

```
class Page extends React.Component {
    constructor(props) {
        super(props);

        this.state = {
            "isEditing": false
        };
    }

    render() {
        if (this.state.isEditing) {
            return <PageEditor
                {...this.props}
                onCancel={this.onCancel.bind(this)}
                />;
        }

        return <PageView
```

```
            {...this.props}
            onPageEdit={this.onEdit.bind(this)}
            />;
    }

    onEdit() {
        this.setState({
            "isEditing": true
        });
    }

    onCancel() {
        this.setState({
            "isEditing": false
        });
    }
}
```

We're providing a way for *child* components to call methods in *parent* components by passing down methods child components can use. When a `PageView` class wants to put the `Page` into edit mode, it can call `this.props.onEdit`. The `Page` will know how to handle that. We'll see this pattern often, so it's good to understand what it's doing here before moving on!

In the same way, we provide a way for a `PageEditor` class to cancel edit mode. In both these cases, we use `setState` to switch between editing and viewing states.

 We bind the handle methods, because otherwise `this` will mean something different when the methods are called. Binding like this is not efficient, so we'll revisit this later with an alternative!

We can connect these handlers to click events in each component:

```
class PageEditor extends React.Component {
    render() {
        return <form>
            <input type="text" name="title" />
            <textarea name="body"></textarea>
            <button>save</button>
            <button
                onClick={this.onCancel.bind(this)}
                >back</button>
        </form>;
    }
```

```
    onCancel(event) {
        event.preventDefault();
        this.props.onCancel();
    }
}
```

We need to prevent default form submission before calling the onCancel passed down through props. The code is as follows:

```
class PageView extends React.Component {
    render() {
        return <div>
            {this.props.title}
            <button
                onClick={this.props.onEdit}
            >edit</button>
            <button>delete</button>
        </div>;
    }
}
```

You should now be able to run this in a browser and toggle between the edit and view aspects of each page. This is a good time to stop and take stock of what we've achieved:

1. We created an entry-point component to page management called PageAdmin. This component handles fetching and persisting page data. It uses a Backend class to do these. It also renders Page components for each page that Backend returns.

2. We created a Page component to encapsulate page data as well as edit and view aspects of each page. The Page component handles switching between these two child components, via callbacks.

3. We created PageEditor as an interface for editing page data. It contains a couple of fields, which we'll shortly discuss.

4. Finally, we created PageView as an interface for viewing page data and getting to the edit mode. We're about to make the **Delete** button work too.

If you've been following along, your interface may look something like this:

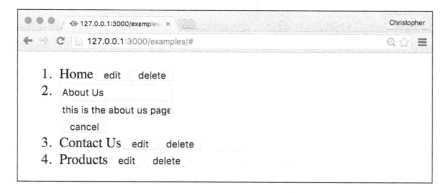

We have created new function references throughout this chapter. Every time we use
fn.bind(this), we create a new function. This is inefficient if we're doing it inside
render methods. We can get around this by creating a base component:

```
import React from "react";

class Component extends React.Component {
    bind(...methods) {
        methods.map(
            method => this[method] = this[method].bind(this)
        )
    }
}

export default Component;
```

If we extend this base component (instead of the usual React.Component), then
we will have access to the bind method. It takes one or more function names, and
replaces them with bound versions.

Now, we need to add event handlers for updating and deleting pages. Let's start
with PageView and PageEditor:

```
import Component from "component";

class PageView extends Component {
    constructor(props) {
        super(props);

        this.bind(
            "onDelete"
```

```
            );
        }

    render() {
        return <div>
            {this.props.title}
            <button
                onClick={this.props.onEdit}
                >edit</button>
            <button
                onClick={this.onDelete}
                >delete</button>
        </div>;
    }

    onDelete() {
        this.props.onDelete(
            this.props.id
        );
    }
}
```

We added an `onClick` handler to the Delete button. This will trigger a bound version of `onDelete` in which we pass the correct:

```
import Component from "component";

class PageEditor extends Component {
    constructor(props) {
        super(props);

        this.bind(
            "onCancel",
            "onUpdate"
        );
    }

    render() {
        return <form>
            <input
                type="text"
                name="title"
                value={this.props.title}
                onChange={this.onUpdate}
```

```
        />
    <textarea
        name="body"
        value={this.props.body}
         onChange={this.onUpdate}>
    </textarea>
    <button
        onClick={this.onCancel}>
        cancel
    </button>
    </div>;
}

onUpdate() {
    this.props.onUpdate(
        this.props.id,
        event.target.name,
        event.target.value
    );
}

onCancel(event) {
    event.preventDefault();
    this.props.onCancel();
}
}
```

Here, we added onUpdate so that we can determine which input changed. It calls the props onUpdate method with the correct property name and value.

We also add the name and value attributes for the inputs, setting the values to the corresponding properties. These updates are triggered when the inputs change, calling the onUpdate method. This means property updates will reflect in the fields.

Where do these new handler properties come from? We need to add them to PageAdmin:

```
import Component from "component";

class PageAdmin extends Component {
    constructor(props) {
        super(props);

        this.state = {
            "pages": []
        };
```

```
        this.bind(
            "onUpdate",
            "onDelete"
        );
    }

    componentWillMount() {
        this.setState({
            "pages": this.props.backend.getAll()
        });
    }

    render() {
        return <ol>
            {this.state.pages.map(function(page) {
                return <li key={page.id}>
                    <Page
                        {...page}
                        onUpdate={this.onUpdate}
                        onDelete={this.onDelete}
                        />
                </li>;
            })}
        </ol>;
    }

    onUpdate(...params) {
        this.props.backend.update(...params);
    }

    onDelete(...params) {
        this.props.backend.delete(...params);
    }
}
```

Finally, we create a couple of methods to handle updates and deletes. These are bound, as we've been doing to methods in the other classes. They also use the rest/spread operators as a bit of a shortcut!

We can fake the backend data and operations with an array of pages and a few array modifier methods:

```
class Backend {
    constructor() {
        this.deleted = [];
```

```
        this.updates = [];

        this.pages = [
            {
                "id": 1,
                "title": "Home",
                "body": "..."
            },
            {
                "id": 2,
                "title": "About Us",
                "body": "..."
            },
            {
                "id": 3,
                "title": "Contact Us",
                "body": "..."
            },
            {
                "id": 4,
                "title": "Products",
                "body": "..."
            }
        ];
    }

getAll() {
    return this.pages
        .filter(page => {
            return this.deleted.indexOf(page.id) == -1
        })
        .map(page => {
            var modified = page;

            this.updates.forEach((update) => {
                if (update[0] == page.id) {
                    modified[update[1]] = update[2];
                }
            });

            return modified;
        });
}
```

```
update(id, property, value) {
    this.updates.push([id, property, value]);
}

delete(id) {
    this.deleted.push(id);
}
}
```

This is by no means an efficient implementation. Please do not use this code in production. It's just an example interface against which we can test our code!

The `all` method returns a filtered and mapped array of initial pages. The `() => {}` syntax is a shortcut for `(function(){}).bind(this)`. The brackets are even optional, if there is exactly one property for the function. The filter checks that each page `id` is not in the `deleted` array. We're not actually deleting pages in this pretend backend. We're simply excluding ones we know we don't want to see.

We don't update the pages directly, but we apply updates to the array before `all` returns it. This isn't efficient, but it does allow us to see out interface in action.

You can learn more about these array tricks at `https://developer.mozilla.org/docs/Web/JavaScript/Reference/Global_Objects/Array`. It's a great place to learn about JavaScript language features.

Component life cycle methods

There are a couple of tricks I want to show you before we wrap up. The first is a *life cycle method* we can use to tell when a component's properties will change. We can use this to change the appearance of a component, or refresh the internal state.

We can add this method to `PageEditor`, for example:

```
class PageEditor extends Component {
    constructor(props) {
        super(props);

        this.state = {
            "changed": false
        };
```

```
        this.bind(
            "onCancel",
            "onUpdate"
        );
    }

    isChanged(next, previous) {
        return JSON.stringify(next) !== JSON.stringify(previous)
    }

    componentWillReceiveProps(props) {
        this.setState({
            "changed": this.isChanged(props, this.props)
        });
    }

    render() {
        return <div>
            <input
                type="text"
                name="title"
                value={this.props.title}
                onChange={this.onUpdate}
                />
            <textarea
                name="body"
                value={this.props.body}
                onChange={this.onUpdate}>
            </textarea>
            <button
                onClick={this.onCancel}>
                cancel
            </button>
        </div>;
    }

    onUpdate() {
        this.props.onUpdate(
            this.props.id,
            event.target.name,
            event.target.value
        );
    }
```

```
        onCancel(event) {
            event.preventDefault();
            this.props.onCancel();
        }
    }
```

We can now tell when the page changes, even though the changes are immediately propagated.

Another magic method we can use will help cut down on the comparisons React needs to perform. It's called shouldComponentUpdate and we can add it to PageView:

```
class PageView extends Component {
    constructor(props) {
        super(props);

        this.bind(
            "onDelete"
        );
    }

    isChanged(next, previous) {
        return JSON.stringify(next) !== JSON.stringify(previous)
    }

    shouldComponentUpdate(props, state) {
        return this.isChanged(props, this.props);
    }

    render() {
        return <div>
            {this.props.title}
            <button
                onClick={this.props.onEdit}
                >edit</button>
            <button
                onClick={this.onDelete}
                >delete</button>
        </div>;
    }

    onDelete() {
        this.props.onDelete(
            this.props.id
        );
    }
}
```

The `shouldComponentUpdate` method gives us a way to tell React not to look for changes in this component. At this scale, we're not likely to see huge performance improvements. But when we add this method to more complex layouts, it will drastically reduce the amount of work required to work out how the document should change.

We'll be using these tricks later, as we build more complex content management features.

Summary

In this chapter, you learned even more about ES6 classes and how they complement React components in structure and functionality. We also looked at some interesting uses of state and properties.

Above all, we saw how it's both possible and beneficial to avoid the internal component state. Properties are a powerful tool for component design. We know how to react to changing properties and how to reduce the work React needs to do to render our interfaces.

In the next chapter, we are going to discuss how to persist this data (to different kinds of local storage). We will see how to connect to these data stores through events.

3
Saving and Communicating Data

In the previous chapter, we created complex component hierarchies. We created a list of pages and a way to edit those pages. Yet we stopped short of saving and reading any of that data to some kind of storage.

We could, for instance, send an edit through an Ajax request to be saved in a database server. In fact, that's what often happens in the applications we use these days. They always save our interactions, irrespective of whether we expect them to or not.

In this chapter, you will learn about local data stores and communicating with them. You'll also learn about event-based architecture and how it promotes the unidirectional flow of data.

There are many ways to save data. It's a rich and interesting topic that could fill scores of books. I could go so far as to say it is at the core of how businesses and applications work.

Furthermore, how data is communicated can often be different in a maintainable application and an unmaintainable application. It's up to us to figure out elegant ways of persisting data so that our applications remain maintainable.

We will only explore local storage in this chapter. You'll be able to see your stored data beyond page reloads, but nobody else will. You cannot build a practical website based on this chapter alone. You will have to wait until we explore React on the server.

Validating properties

Before we look at storing data, there is another habit I'd like to share with you. The components we created in the last chapter work well together, but our aim is to make each component self-contained. We want others to be able to reuse our components, but they will encounter problems if they don't know which properties our components expect.

Consider what would happen if we used `PageAdmin` like this:

```
ReactDOM.render(
    <PageAdmin backend="ajax" />,
    document.querySelector(".react")
);
```

Faced with this component, and no documentation, it might be tempting to substitute a `Backend` object with some other configuration data. This looks reasonable to someone unfamiliar with the component. And, without a careful study of all our components, we can't expect others to know what those properties should be.

We can protect against this situation by adding property validation. Let's add some validation to `PageEditor`:

```
PageEditor.propTypes = {
    "id": React.PropTypes.number.isRequired,
    "title": React.PropTypes.string.isRequired,
    "body": React.PropTypes.string.isRequired,
    "onUpdate": React.PropTypes.func.isRequired,
    "onCancel": React.PropTypes.func.isRequired
};
```

We have already imported the `React` object, which exposes a `PropTypes` object. This contains some validators. When we specify a few on `PageEditor.propTypes`, React checks the types of properties given to the component as it is rendered. If we give the incorrect property types or omit required properties, React will emit a warning.

The warnings look like this:

```
⊗ ▶Warning: Failed propType: Required prop `id` was not specified in `PageEditor`.          react.js:18745
⊗ ▶Warning: Failed propType: Required prop `title` was not specified in `PageEditor`.        react.js:18745
⊗ ▶Warning: Failed propType: Required prop `body` was not specified in `PageEditor`.         react.js:18745
⊗ ▶Warning: Failed propType: Required prop `onPageUpdate` was not specified in `PageEditor`. react.js:18745
⊗ ▶Warning: Failed propType: Required prop `onPageCancel` was not specified in `PageEditor`. react.js:18745
```

There are many types to choose from, the simple ones being the following:

- `React.PropTypes.array`
- `React.PropTypes.bool`
- `React.PropTypes.func`
- `React.PropTypes.number`
- `React.PropTypes.object`
- `React.PropTypes.string`

If you need a property to be required (which is likely in most cases) then you can add `.isRequired` at the end. Let's follow this up with validators for `PageView`:

```
PageView.propTypes = {
    "title": React.PropTypes.string.isRequired,
    "onEdit": React.PropTypes.func.isRequired,
    "onDelete": React.PropTypes.func.isRequired
};
```

This is even simpler, given that `PageView` uses fewer properties than `PageEditor`. Also, `Page` is relatively simple:

```
Page.propTypes = {
    "id": React.PropTypes.number.isRequired,
    "onDelete": React.PropTypes.func.isRequired
};
```

We don't need to validate properties passed straight through components. For instance, `PageEditor` uses `onUpdate`. It's passed through `Page`, but `Page` doesn't use it, `PageEditor` does, so that's where we use validators for it.

However, what if we want to validate nested structures or more complex types? We can try the following:

```
PageAdmin.propTypes = {
    "backend": function(props, propName, componentName) {
        if (props.backend instanceof Backend) {
            return;
        }

        return new Error(
            "Required prop `backend` is not a `Backend`."
        );
    }
};
```

We expect the `backend` property to be an instance of the `Backend` class. If it is anything else, we return an `Error` describing why the property is invalid. We can also use `shape` to validate nested properties:

```
Component.propTypes = {
    "page": React.PropTypes.shape({
        "id": React.PropTypes.number.isRequired,
        "title": React.PropTypes.string.isRequired,
        "body": React.PropTypes.string.isRequired
    })
};
```

The more specific we are about properties, the less chance there is for bad properties to break the interface. So, it's good to get in the habit of defining them all the time.

Storing cookies

You must have heard of cookies before. They're a browser-based storage mechanism as old as the Internet, and they are often comically described in movies. Here's how we use them:

```
document.cookie = "pages=all_the_pages";
document.cookie = "current=current_page_id";
```

The `document.cookie` parameter works as a temporary string store. You can keep adding new strings, where the key and value are separated by =, and they will be stored beyond a page reload, that is, until you reach the limit of how many cookies your browser will store per domain. If you set `document.cookie` multiple times, multiple cookies will be set.

You can read the cookies back again, with a function like this:

```
var cookies = {};

function readCookie(name) {
    var chunks = document.cookie.split("; ");

    for (var i = chunks.length - 1; i >= 0; i--) {
        var parts = chunks[i].split("=");
        cookies[parts[0]] = parts[1];
    }

    return cookies[name];
}

export default readCookie;
```

The whole cookie string is read and split using semicolons. Then, each cookie is split into equals, leaving the key and value. These are stored in the local `cookies` object. Future requests just read the key from the local object. The `cookies` object can be inspected at any point to see the cookies that have been set.

Try `http://browsercookielimits.squawky.net` to test what your browser can handle. I'm running a modern version of Chrome, and I can probably store 180 cookies per domain, totaling 4096 bytes. 4096 bytes doesn't sound like a lot...

Cookies aren't typically used for the kinds of data we want to store. We'll have to look elsewhere.

 If you want to learn more about how to use cookies, head over to `https://developer.mozilla.org/en-US/docs/Web/API/Document/cookie`.

Using local storage

The next type of storage we will look at is a relatively recent addition to the browser toolset. It's called *local storage*, and it's been around for a while. You can add items to it as follows:

```
localStorage.setItem("pages", "all_the_pages");
```

It's simpler than cookies to read items from:

```
localStorage.getItem("pages");
```

This will persist the data beyond page reloads or the browser closing. You can store considerably more data than in cookies (anywhere from 3 MB to 10 MB, by default), and the interface is easier to use.

So, how can we use this to store our pages? Let's abstract local storage a bit:

```
export default {
    "get": function(key, defaultValue) {
        var value = window.localStorage.getItem(key);

        var decoded = JSON.parse(value);

        if (decoded) {
            return decoded;
        }
```

```
        return defaultValue;
    },

    "set": function(key, value) {
        window.localStorage.setItem(
            key, JSON.stringify(value)
        );
    }
};
```

For once, we're exporting an object instead of a class. This object has a couple of methods both of which access window.localStorage. It's not ideal to reference this directly, but if we use this abstraction everywhere else, then I think it's OK.

The get method pulls a string value out of local storage and parses it as a JSON string. If the value parses to any non-false value, we return it, or else we return a default value.

The set method encodes a value as JSON, and stores it.

Then, we can use the following abstraction in the Backend class:

```
import LocalStore from "local-store";

class Backend {
    constructor() {
        this.pages = LocalStore.get("pages", []);
    }

    getAll() {
        return this.pages;
    }

    update(id, property, value) {
        this.pages = this.pages.map((page) => {
            if (page.id == id) {
                page[property] = value;
            }

            return page;
        });

        LocalStore.set("pages", this.pages);
    }
```

```
    delete(id) {
        this.pages = this.pages.filter(
            (page) => page.id !== id
        );

        LocalStore.set("pages", this.pages);
    }
}

export default Backend;
```

We begin with a constructor that fetches any stored pages from localStorage. We provide a default empty array in case the pages key is missing in localStorage. We store that in this.pages so we can fetch and modify it later.

The getAll method is much simpler this time around. All it does is returns this. pages. The update and delete methods become more interesting though. The update method uses the Array.map method to apply updates to the affected page objects. We have to store the updated pages array back in local storage so that the changes are persisted.

Similarly, delete modifies the pages array (this time with a short function syntax) and stores the modified array back in local storage. We have to see local storage with some initial data. You can do this in a developer console:

```
localStorage.setItem("pages", JSON.stringify([
    {
        "id": 1,
        "title": "Home",
        "body": "..."
    },
    {
        "id": 2,
        "title": "About Us",
        "body": "..."
    },
    {
        "id": 3,
        "title": "Contact Us",
        "body": "..."
    },
    {
        "id": 4,
        "title": "Products",
```

```
        "body": "..."
    }
]));
```

If you've made these changes, and you refresh the page, you should see the new backend code in action!

Using event emitters

Until now, our components have communicated with the backend through method calls. That's OK for tiny applications, but when things start to scale, we will forget to make some of those method calls.

Look at onUpdate, for instance:

```
onUpdate(id, field, value) {
    this.props.backend.update(id, field, value);

    this.setState({
        "pages": this.props.backend.getAll()
    });
}
```

Every time we change the state of a page, we have to fetch an updated list of pages from the backend. What if multiple components send updates to the backend? How will our PageAdmin component know when to fetch a new list of pages?

We can turn to event-based architecture to solve this problem. We've already encountered and used events! Recollect what we did when we created the page edit form. There, we connected to input events so we could update pages when input values changed.

This kind of architecture moves us closer to a unidirectional flow of data. We can imagine our entire application like a tree of components, beginning with a single root component. When a component needs to update some application's state, we don't need to code the state change in relation to where that component is. In the past, we may have had to reference specific CSS selectors, or depend on the position of sibling elements, when updating state.

When we start to use events, then any component can trigger a change in the application. Also, multiple components can trigger the same kind of change. We'll explore this idea in more detail in later chapters.

We can use that same idea to notify components when the data changes. To begin with, we need to download an event emitter class:

```
$ npm install --save eventemitter3
```

Now, Backend can extend this, providing the event functionality that we are after:

```
class Backend extends EventEmitter {
    constructor() {
        super();

        this.pages = LocalStore.get("pages", []);
    }

    getAll() {
        return this.pages;
    }

    update(id, property, value) {
        // ...update a page

        this.emit("update", this.pages);
    }

    delete(id) {
        // ...delete a page

        this.emit("update", this.pages);
    }
}
```

As each page is updated or deleted, the backend will emit an event on itself. This does nothing until we listen for these events in PageAdmin:

```
constructor(props) {
    super(props);

    this.bind(
        "onUpdate",
        "onDelete"
    );

    this.state = {
        "pages": this.props.backend.getAll()
    };
```

```
        this.props.backend.on("update",
            (pages) => this.setState({pages})
        );
    }

onUpdate(id, field, value) {
    this.props.backend.update(id, field, value);
}

onDelete(id) {
    this.props.backend.delete(id);
}
```

Now we can remove the numerous calls to `this.setState` and replace them with a single event listener in the `constructor`. We are also doing something interesting with the `setState` call. It's called *object destructuring*, and it allows `{pages}` to become `{"pages":pages}`.

Now we can begin to use this backend for many different parts of the interface, and they'll all have accurate, real-time data. Open the page up in a few different windows and watch them all update at once!

Summary

In this chapter, we looked at how to protect our components from faulty properties. We also saw how easy it was to use cookies, although they are limited for what we need. Fortunately, we can use local storage and work it into our existing backend and components.

Finally, we explored using events to push state changes out to all interested components.

In the next chapter, we will start prettying up our components. We'll look at ways to style and animate them, bringing our interface to life!

4
Styling and Animating Components

In the last chapter, you learned how persist pages even after reloading the page or restarting the browser. We're at the point now where this could start to be a useful system for us. Unfortunately, it still looks rough and unstyled.

That's because, up until now, we've almost completely ignored styles in our components. In this chapter, we will change all that!

You will learn how to add custom styles and class names to component elements. We'll add animations to new and old components. We'll even learn how to combine the two to create highly reusable styles and animation.

Adding new pages

So far, we are able to change and remove pages from our content management system. We ended the last chapter by seeding our local storage with a serialized array, so we could see it in action. Let's take a step back and make a way to create new pages through the interface.

First, we'll add an `insert` method and update the `constructor` method of `Backend`:

```
constructor() {
    super();

    var pages = LocalStore.get("pages", []);

    this.id = 1;

    this.pages = pages.map((page) => {
```

```
            page.id = this.id++;
            return page;
        });
    }

    insert() {
        this.pages.push({
            "id": this.id,
            "title": "New page " + this.id,
            "body": ""
        });

        this.id++;

        LocalStore.set("pages", this.pages);

        this.emit("update", this.pages);
    }
```

The page `id` values aren't really important to us outside the context of our React components. So, it's fine to regenerate them as the pages are loaded from local storage. We keep track of the internal `id` value, so new pages can be assigned a new `id` value when they are created.

The `insert` method pushes a new page object onto the list of pages. We then update the `pages` data in local storage so it's available the next time we need the pages. And, as with the `update` and `delete` methods, we emit an `update` event, so all concerned components will update their state.

We can use this `insert` method in `PageAdmin`:

```
onInsert() {
    this.props.backend.insert();
}
```

In the `render` method, add the following code:

```
render() {
    return <div>
        <div>
            <button onClick={this.onInsert}>
                create new page
            </button>
        </div>
        <ol>
```

```
            . . .
        </ol>
    </div>;
}
```

Along with the rest of the code we wrote, the interface looks like this:

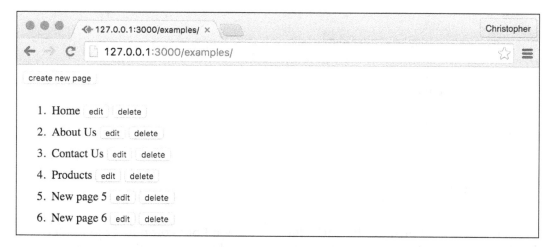

Adding styles to components

There are a number of ways we could improve the appearance of our components. Let's take the `PageView` component, for example. What would make it better? Perhaps if we increased the font size and used a sans serif font, the titles would be clearer to read. Perhaps we could increase the margin around each page.

There are a few different ways to style our components. The first is by adding styles inline to the `render` method in `PageView`:

```
render() {
    var rowStyle = this.props.rowStyle || {
        "fontSize": "18px",
        "fontFamily": "Helvetica"
    };

    var labelStyle = this.props.labelStyle || {
        "whiteSpace": "nowrap"
    };

    var buttonStyle = this.props.buttonStyle || {
        "margin": "0 0 0 10px",
```

```
            "verticalAlign": "middle",
        };

        return <div style={rowStyle}>
            <label style={labelStyle}>
                {this.props.title}
            </label>
            <button
                style={buttonStyle}
                onClick={this.props.onEdit}>
                edit
            </button>
            <button
                style={buttonStyle}
                onClick={this.props.onDelete}>
                delete
            </button>
        </div>;
    }
```

We can define a set of styles for each element we want our component to render. For the outer `div` element, we define a font size and family. For the `label` title, we tell the browser not to wrap text. For each button, we add margins. Each style object may be overwritten through properties, owing to the `var value = value1 ||` `value2` notation. That's shorthand for saying if `value1` is undefined, use `value2`.

We should also apply those styles to the list items, so the numbers appear in the same manner as the titles:

```
render() {
    var itemStyle = this.props.itemStyle || {
        "minHeight": "40px",
        "lineHeight": "40px",
        "fontSize": "18px",
        "fontFamily": "Helvetica"

    };

    return <div>
        <div>
            <button
                onClick={this.onInsert}>
                create new page
            </button>
        </div>
```

```
    <ol>
        {this.state.pages.map((page, i) => {
            return <li key={i} style={itemStyle}>
                <Page
                    {...page}
                    onUpdate={this.onUpdate}
                    onDelete={this.onDelete}
                    />);
            </li>;
        })}
    </ol>
</div>;
}
```

Note how there are two sets of braces for the `style` object? That's how we define objects as properties. In this case, it's an object of styles we want applied to each list item.

Changing and reverting

Now we can style our edit form. Let's replace the modification indicator (asterisk) with a button that will simulate the save action:

```
constructor(props) {
    super(props);

    this.state = {
        "changed": false
    };

    this.bind(
        "onCancel",
        "onSave",
        "onUpdate",
    );
}

render() {
    var cancelButtonStyle = null;
    var saveButton = null;

    if (this.state.changed) {
        cancelButtonStyle = this.props.cancelButtonStyle || {
```

```
            "margin": "0 0 0 10px"
        };

        saveButton = <button
            onClick={this.onCancel}>
            save
        </button>
    }

    return <form>
        <div>
            <input
                type="text"
                onChange={this.onUpdate}
                name="title"
                value={this.props.title}
                />
        </div>
        <div>
            <input
                type="text"
                onChange={this.onUpdate}
                name="body"
                value={this.props.body}
                />
        </div>
        {saveButton}
        <button
            onClick={this.onCancel}
            style={cancelButtonStyle}>
            cancel
        </button>
    </form>;
}

onSave(event) {
    event.perventDefault();
    this.props.onSave();
}
```

This gives the illusion that clicking on the **Save** button will save something, when the save happens regardless. This poses an interesting question—should we make the **Cancel** button cancel the edit? Because right now it's just a back button masquerading as a cancel button. We should also define an `onSave` function to pass to this component.

To do that, we'd have to track its initial state. But where would we get this initial state? The `PageEditor` component receives the page details through properties, so the current state is the same in `PageEditor` as it is in `Backend`.

Perhaps we should store the state when `PageView` is hidden and `PageEditor` is shown:

```
onEdit() {
    this.setState({
        "isEditing": true,
        "title": this.props.title
    });
}
```

When the page enters edit mode, we store the unedited title. We should change the `onCancel` method to actually cancel a change:

```
onCancel() {
    this.props.onUpdate(
        this.props.id,
        "title",
        this.state.title
    );

    this.setState({
        "isEditing": false
    });
}

onSave() {
    this.setState({
        "isEditing": false
    });
}
```

When the `onCancel` property is called, we set the page title to the unedited title we stored earlier. We need to bind this new `onSave` method in the constructor:

```
constructor(props) {
    super(props);

    this.state = {
        "isEditing": false
    };

    this.bind(
        "onEdit",
        "onDelete",
        "onCancel",
        "onSave"
    );
}
```

This assures that `this` refers to the page component when the `onSave` property is later called. We'll need to pass this new method to the `PageEditor` component in the form of a property:

```
render() {
    if (this.state.isEditing) {
        return <PageEditor
            {...this.props}
            onCancel={this.onCancel}
            onSave={this.onSave}
            />;
    }

    return <PageView
        {...this.props}
        onEdit={this.onEdit}
        onDelete={this.onDelete}
        />;
}
```

Now, instead of both the `PageEditor` buttons calling `this.props.onCancel`, they can call their applicable methods:

```
if (this.state.changed) {
    cancelButtonStyle = this.props.cancelButtonStyle || {
        "margin": "0 0 0 10px"
    };
```

```
saveButton = <button
    onClick={this. onSave}>
    save
</button>
}
```

Animating new components

At the moment, new pages are just appearing. There's no subtle animation to ease them in. Let's change that!

We will use a new React component for this, and we can find it in the add-ons build of React. Go back to the React scripts you downloaded in the first chapter and replace all references to react.js with react-with-addons.js.

This gives us access to a new component called CSSTransitionGroup:

```
render() {
    var itemStyle = this.props.itemStyle || {
        "minHeight": "40px",
        "lineHeight": "40px",
        "fontSize": "18px",
        "fontFamily": "Helvetica"
    };

    return <div>
        <div>
            <button
                onClick={this.onInsert}>
                create new page
            </button>
        </div>
        <ol>
            <React.addons.CSSTransitionGroup
                transitionName="page"
                transitionEnterTimeout={150}
                transitionLeaveTimeout={150}>
                {this.state.pages.map((page, i) => {
                    return <li key={i} style={itemStyle}>
                        <Page
                            {...page}
                            onUpdate={this.onUpdate}
```

```
                                onDelete={this.onDelete}
                                />
                        </li>;
                    })}
                </React.addons.CSSTransitionGroup>
            </ol>
        </div>;
    }
```

This new container component watches for changes in its children. When new child components are added, they are given a couple of CSS class names, which can apply CSS animation. We need to add this animation to the corresponding CSS styles:

```
.page-enter {
    opacity: 0.01;
    margin-left: -50%;
}

.page-enter.page-enter-active {
    opacity: 1;
    margin-left: 0;
    transition: all 150ms linear;
}

.page-leave {
    opacity: 1;
    margin-left: 0;
}

.page-leave.page-leave-active {
    opacity: 0.01;
    margin-left: 50%;
    transition: all 150ms linear;
}
```

Since we specified `transitionName="page"`, React adds `page-enter` and `page-leave` to the `Page` components, as they enter and leave `PageAdmin`. Note how `150ms` in our styles matches `transitionEnterTimeout={150}`? They need to be the same. React adds classes such as `page-enter-active` for those `150ms`, and then removes them. This ensures that transitions only happen once.

Working with CSS transitions

It's a great time to talk about CSS transitions. We have used them to fade and slide new `Page` components in from the left. If you're unfamiliar with how they generally work, the code might be confusing and difficult to change.

There are a few things you should know. The first is that you can transition individual CSS properties or all of them at once:

```
.background-transition {
    background-color: red;
    font-size: 16px;
    transition-property: background-color;
}

.background-transition:hover {
    background: blue;
    font-size: 18px;
}
```

In this example, we only want to transition the background color. The font size will immediately jump from `16px` to `18px`. Alternatively, we can transition all CSS properties:

```
.all-transition {
    transition-property: all;
}
```

We've already seen transition duration, albeit briefly. We can use `ms` or `s` as units for these:

```
.background-transition {
    transition-duration: 1s;
}
```

Then there are timing functions. These control how the animation gets from 0% to 100%. They're sometimes called curves because of how they're often demonstrated:

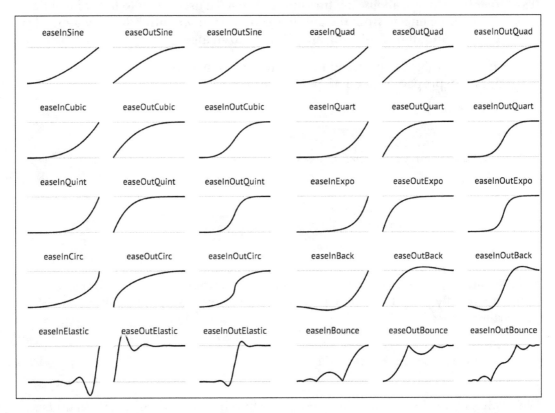

Linear is the most basic of these timing functions, moving evenly from 0% to 100%. It's also the default `timing` function.

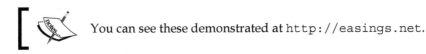

You can see these demonstrated at http://easings.net.

You can also define your own curve, in the `cubic-bezier(x1, y1, x2, y2)` form. That's a bit advanced for now, but it's good to know in any case.

Transitions can also be delayed, so they only happen after the desired amount of time:

```
.background-transition {
    transition-delay: 1s;
}
```

Altogether, these styles look like this:

```
.background-transition {
    transition-property: background;
    transition-duration: 1s;
    transition-timing-function: linear;
    transition-delay: 0.5s;
}
```

As in the previous section, you can bundle all of these properties together into a smaller set:

```
.background-transition {
    transition: background 1s linear 0.5s;
}
```

Not all properties can be transitioned. Properties need to have some form of granularity. Some common properties are as follows:

- background (applies to color and position)
- border (applies to color, width, and spacing)
- bottom
- clip
- color
- crop
- font (applies to size and weight)
- height
- left
- letter-spacing
- line-height
- margin
- max-height
- max-width
- min-height
- min-width
- opacity
- outline (applies to color, offset, and width)
- padding
- right

- `text-indent`
- `text-shadow`
- `top`
- `vertical-align`
- `visibility`
- `width`
- `word-spacing`
- `z-index`

Organizing styles with Sass

Style sheets are a great alternative to inline component styles. CSS is wonderfully expressive as a language for finding and applying visual characteristics to elements.

Unfortunately, it also has drawbacks. The biggest drawback to CSS is that all styles are in global scope. Some styles are inherited, and styles applied to elements often collide (and cancel each other out).

In small doses, the collisions are avoidable or manageable. In large doses, these collisions can cripple productivity. As a stop-gap, CSS supports the `!important` keyword. This often leads to ugly hacks, as everyone wants their styles to be the most important.

In addition to this, common values need to be repeated. Until recently, CSS didn't even support calculated values. If we wanted an element to have an absolute width (for example) in relation to other elements, we had to use JavaScript.

These are some of the problems Sass aims to solve. It's a CSS superset language (CSS + other features), so it's easy to learn, that is, once you know CSS.

Sass style sheets need to be compiled to CSS style sheets before they can be used in the browser. Installing a Sass compiler is easy; execute the following command to install it:

```
$ npm install --save node-sass
```

After that's done, we're able to compile Sass style sheets (files ending in `.scss`) with the following:

```
$ node_modules/.bin/node-sass index.scss > index.css
```

Consider the following code:

```
$duration: 150ms;
$timing-function: linear;

.page-enter {
    opacity: 0.01;
    margin-left: -50%;

    &.page-enter-active {
        opacity: 1;
        margin-left: 0;
        transition: all $duration $timing-function;
    }
}

.page-leave {
    opacity: 1;
    margin-left: 0;

    &.page-leave-active {
        opacity: 0.01;
        margin-left: 50%;
        transition: all $duration $timing-function;
    }
}
```

The preceding code will be turned into CSS, as follows:

```
.page-enter {
    opacity: 0.01;
    margin-left: -50%;
}

.page-enter.page-enter-active {
    opacity: 1;
    margin-left: 0;
    transition: all 150ms linear;
}

.page-leave {
    opacity: 1;
    margin-left: 0;
}
```

```
.page-leave.page-leave-active {
    opacity: 0.01;
    margin-left: 50%;
    transition: all 150ms linear;
}
```

If you prefer to compile React components in the browser and want to do the same with Sass, then you can install the following:

```
$ npm install --save sass.js
```

Then, you need to add the following elements to the head of your page:

```
<script src="/node_modules/sass.js/dist/sass.sync.js"></script>
<style type="text/sass">
    $duration: 150ms;
    $timing-function: linear;

    .page-enter {
        opacity: 0.01;
        margin-left: -50%;

        &.page-enter-active {
            opacity: 1;
            margin-left: 0;
            transition: all $duration $timing-function;
        }
    }

    .page-leave {
        opacity: 1;
        margin-left: 0;

        &.page-leave-active {
            opacity: 0.01;
            margin-left: 50%;
            transition: all $duration $timing-function;
        }
    }
</style>
<script>
    var stylesheets = Array.prototype.slice.call(
        document.querySelectorAll("[type='text/sass']")
    );
```

```
    stylesheets.forEach(function(stylesheet) {
        Sass.compile(stylesheet.innerHTML, function(result) {
            stylesheet.type = "text/css";
            stylesheet.innerHTML = result.text;
        });
    });
</script>
```

This is a bit of JavaScript to look for the `style` elements with `type="text/sass"`. The contents of each of these style elements is passed through `sass.js` and saved back into the style elements. Their type is changed back to `text/css`, so the browser will recognize the styles as CSS.

 You should only use this method in development. It creates a lot of work for the browser, which can be avoided by pre-compiling Sass for a production environment (using tools such as Grunt, Gulp, and webpack).

Alternatives

There are a few other ways in which we can style and animate React components, and they all deal with the issue in subtly different ways.

CSS modules

CSS modules allow you to define styles that only apply in a local context to individual elements. They look like regular CSS styles, but when they're applied to components, they are altered so that the class names given to components are unique. You can read more about CSS modules at `http://glenmaddern.com/articles/css-modules`.

React style

React style is a way of creating inline styles as slightly enhanced objects. It lacks support for a few common CSS selectors, but does a good job otherwise. You can read more about it at `https://github.com/js-next/react-style`.

Summary

In this chapter, you learned how to style React components great and small. We used inline styles, CSS style sheets, and even Sass style sheets. You also learned how to animate child components in and out of view using CSS transitions.

Finally, we looked briefly at a couple of alternative technologies, which do the same things we did in this chapter but in slightly different ways. You may prefer one of these methods over all the others, but what is important is to recognize that there are many methods we can use to style and animate components.

In the next chapter, we will put all these skills to use as we dive into material design. There's lots of styling and animation to come!

5
Going Material!

In the last chapter, we looked at the basics of how to style and animate React components. We can make components look how we want them to, but how do we want them to look?

In this chapter, we will look at something called material design. You'll learn how to express our interface not only in terms of components, but in a consistent design language.

You will see a major intersection between component-based design and visual design patterns. Material design is very detailed, as we'll see in this chapter. It describes, in great detail, how each type of component (or surface) must look, feel, and move. It's that core approach of designing in the smallest terms that we've come to understand with React. Now, we get to apply those lessons from a visual standpoint as well.

Understanding material design

For me, the name material design evokes an image of fashion or engineering, where different textures and patterns have distinct visual or technical characteristics. Everything I touch is some kind of material. Everything I see is some kind of material. All of these materials obey the laws of physics and behave in familiar ways.

These senses, of touch and sight, are fundamental to how we interact with the world. They're a broad and unspoken constant. Material design is a language that aims to bridge the gap between the physical and digital world, using material as a metaphor.

In this language, the surfaces and edges of material give us some visual interface cues that are grounded in reality. In this language, components respond immediately to touch in ways that hint at what they can do.

Material design is heavily inspired by print design. Yet all the typography, color, and imagery do more than just look good. They create focus, hierarchy, and meaning. It reinforces the user as the primary cause of movement, using meaningful motion to focus on important areas of the interface, always giving the appropriate amount of feedback.

Surfaces

Each object is represented by a material surface. These objects are sized in **device-independent pixels** (or **dp**, for short). This is a great unit to measure user input because it allows designers to design interfaces independent of the screen size.

It can also be converted to absolute units (such as inches or millimeters) depending on the device's screen size.

 You can learn more about dp at `http://en.wikipedia.org/wiki/Device_independent_pixel`.

Surfaces are thought of as 3D objects, having width, height, and depth. All surfaces have a depth of 1 dp, but they can have any width or height. Surfaces also overlap, so they have a vertical offset from each other.

This vertical offset (or elevation) allows layering, creating a sense of depth similar to the real world. The content on a surface, such as typography and images, lies flat on the surface. Think of it like ink on paper, where the paper has a depth that's easier to notice than the ink printed on it.

This layering effect is accentuated with shadows cast onto lower surfaces. The screen serves as a light source, so the closer the surfaces are to it (the higher they are in the interface), the bigger the shadow they cast.

 You can learn more about elevation and layering at `https://www.google.com/design/spec/what-is-material/elevation-shadows.html`.

Interactions

Surfaces provide the depth and hierarchy, but the real value of an application comes from the content presented through the interface. Content drives interaction.

Material surfaces should respond to interactions. Playing videos, zooming photos, or completing forms should feel natural. An interaction should feel natural, and wherever possible, it should mimic how it would feel in the real world.

 You can learn more about interactions at https://www.google.com/design/spec/animation/responsive-interaction.html.

Motion

One of the ways in which an interface can respond to a user interaction is through the efficient use of motion. Animation is not new to mobile interfaces (where material design was born), but we're talking about a considered approach to how that animation is performed.

Just like in the real world, some objects move faster or slower when interacted with as concepts such as friction and momentum come into play. Some elements compress deeper when pressed and others barely move at all.

 You can learn more about motion at https://www.google.com/design/spec/animation/meaningful-transitions.html.

Typography and iconography

There are guidelines for how to structure and color textual content in material interfaces. Most of the examples show Roboto (which is the standard Android font), but the rules work just as well with other clear typefaces.

Similarly, there are guidelines for how to create and use icons through your interface. There is a standard set of icons (called system icons), which will get you started.

 You can download Roboto from https://www.google.com/fonts/specimen/Roboto and the system icons from http://www.google.com/design/spec/style/icons.html#icons-system-icons.

Keeping your head above water

The first time you read through the material design specification (available at `http://www.google.com/design/spec/material-design/introduction.html`), you may be a little overwhelmed. There's a lot of detail in there, and knowing where to start is not easy.

The truth is you don't have to keep all of it in mind. I freaked out the first time I read through it, but I've since come to realize that the point is not to memorize it all. Sure, that would help when making every minute choice about your interface, but it isn't meant to be a toolkit or component library.

Material design is a language—a living document. Google has and will continue to adapt it, and when you learn a language, it helps to know some of the words. However, you cannot learn a whole language in a day, nor can you learn it well only by memorizing set phrases.

No, to learn a language, you need to speak it daily. You need to take to heart the grammar and struggle through your mistakes, until one day you have learned how to be comfortable with it without consciously having to remember each and every rule. On that day, material design becomes second nature to you.

I encourage you to read through the material design specification at least once before continuing. Remember, you can find it at `http://www.google.com/design/spec/material-design/introduction.html`. It doesn't matter if you forget some or even most of it. The purpose of reading it is that some of the decisions will seem more natural to you, as you remember parts of the specification. The pieces may fit together easier.

Material design lite

Having said all that, there are a few tools to help you get started. The first tool we will look at is called material design lite. Over 120 contributors have teamed up to create a set of reusable components in the material design language.

The *lite* part of the name comes mainly from two things:

- It is framework agnostic, which means you can use it without including something such as jQuery or Angular
- When it is gzipped, it's less than 30 KB

Let's try it out by customizing the colors of the default template. Go to `http://www.getmdl.io/customize/index.html` and pick a couple of colors. The color palettes in material design consist of primary colors and an accent color. You can also use some hues of the primary color in your design, but we'll not worry about those just yet.

As you select colors from the color wheel, you may notice some of the other colors disappear. The color wheel hides colors that will not have enough contrast to those you have already selected.

You should pick the colors you want to use in your design. I've picked the two colors marked as **1** and **2** in the following screenshot:

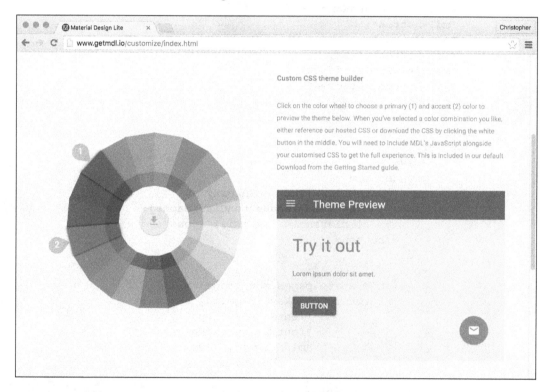

Just below the wheel, you'll see a link element. This points to a hosted CSS file. If you place it in the head of your HTML page, those colors will be applied to your material design elements. I picked indigo and pink, which is reflected in the URL:

```
<link rel="stylesheet" href="https://storage.googleapis.com/code.
getmdl.io/1.0.6/material.indigo-pink.min.css" />
```

You can choose to save this file and serve it locally. For now, I will include it directly in the head of my HTML page.

We also need to include a JavaScript file, and another CSS file that defines a few custom fonts:

```
<script src="https://storage.googleapis.com/code.getmdl.io/1.0.6/
material.min.js"></script>
<link rel="stylesheet" href="https://fonts.googleapis.com/
icon?family=Material+Icons">
```

Let's add a few class names to our button elements as we begin to apply some material design styles to our interface. We'll begin with PageAdmin:

```
render() {
    var addButton ClassNames = [
        "mdl-button",
        "mdl-js-button",
        "mdl-button--fab",
        "mdl-js-ripple-effect",
        "mdl-button--colored"
    ].join(" ");

    return (
        <div>
            <div>
                <button
                    onClick={this.onInsert}
                    className={addButtonClassNames}>
                    <i className="material-icons">add</i>
                </button>
            </div>
            <ol>
                {this.state.pages.map((page) => {
                    return <li key={page.id} style={{
                            "fontSize": "18px",
                            "fontFamily": "Helvetica",
                            "minHeight": "40px",
                            "lineHeight": "40px"
                        }}>
                        <Page
                            {...page}
                            onUpdate={this.onUpdate}
                            onDelete={this.onDelete} />
                    </li>;
                })}
            </ol>
        </div>
    );
}
```

All the material design lite class names start with `mdl-`. We added a few that define some visual styles for **floating action buttons** (or **FAB**, for short).

These styles make our *add* button look much better:

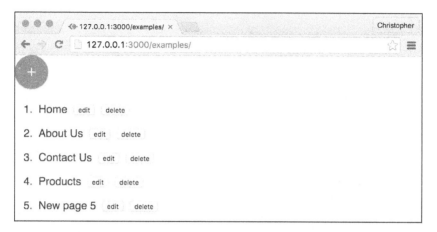

This isn't a great layout though. We should position the button better and add some boundaries to the `Page` components. In fact, we should start thinking of this CMS interface in terms of the different sections/pages we plan to have.

In the beginning, this admin interface won't be open for everyone to see, so perhaps we should have a login page. And, how will we navigate between different sections of this interface? Perhaps we should add some navigation to the mix.

When we visit `http://www.getmdl.io/templates/index.html`, we can see a few different starter layouts that we can use. I really like the look of the **Dashboard** layout, so I think we can base the navigation on that.

Then, there's the **Text-heavy webpage** layout, which has a list of card components. These look just right for our `Page` components. Let's get to work!

Creating a login page

We'll start by creating a simple login without any server-side validation (for now). We'll break it out into its own `login.html` page and `login.js` file:

```
<!DOCTYPE html>
<html>
    <head>
        <script src="/node_modules/babel-core/browser.js"></script>
        <script src="/node_modules/systemjs/dist/system.js"></script>
```

```
            <script src="https://storage.googleapis.com/code.getmdl.
        io/1.0.6/material.min.js"></script>
            <link rel="stylesheet" href="https://storage.googleapis.com/
        code.getmdl.io/1.0.6/material.indigo-pink.min.css" />
            <link rel="stylesheet" href="https://fonts.googleapis.com/
        icon?family=Material+Icons" />
            <link rel="stylesheet" href="example.css" />
        </head>
        <body class="
            mdl-demo
            mdl-color--grey-100
            mdl-color-text--grey-700
            mdl-base">
            <div class="react"></div>
            <script>
                System.config({
                    "transpiler": "babel",
                    "map": {
                        "react": "/examples/react/react",
                        "react-dom": "/examples/react/react-dom"
                    },
                    "baseURL": "../",
                    "defaultJSExtensions": true
                });

                System.import("examples/login");
            </script>
        </body>
    </html>
```

I made a few changes to how SystemJS is configured. Instead of listing every individual file, we now set the root directory as the `baseURL`. This means we need to change how we import everything except `react` and `react-dom`:

```
import React from "react";
import ReactDOM from "react-dom";
import Nav from "src/nav";
import Login from "src/login";

var layoutClassNames = [
    "demo-layout",
    "mdl-layout",
    "mdl-js-layout",
    "mdl-layout--fixed-drawer"
].join(" ");
```

```
ReactDOM.render(
    <div className={layoutClassNames}>
        <Nav />
        <Login />
    </div>,
    document.querySelector(".react")
);
```

Again, we will use some material design lite **Dashboard** class names, which we defined in example.css:

```css
html, body {
    font-family: "Roboto", "Helvetica", sans-serif;
}

.demo-avatar {
    width: 48px;
    height: 48px;
    border-radius: 24px;
}

.demo-layout .mdl-layout__header .mdl-layout__drawer-button {
    color: rgba(0, 0, 0, 0.54);
}

.mdl-layout__drawer .avatar {
    margin-bottom: 16px;
}

.demo-drawer {
    border: none;
    position: fixed;
}

.demo-drawer .mdl-menu__container {
    z-index: -1;
}

.demo-drawer .demo-navigation {
    z-index: -2;
}

.demo-drawer .mdl-menu .mdl-menu__item {
    display: -webkit-box;
```

```
        display: -webkit-flex;
        display: -ms-flexbox;
        display: flex;
        -webkit-box-align: center;
        -webkit-align-items: center;
        -ms-flex-align: center;
        align-items: center;
    }

    .demo-drawer-header {
        box-sizing: border-box;
        display: -webkit-box;
        display: -webkit-flex;
        display: -ms-flexbox;
        display: flex;
        -webkit-box-orient: vertical;
        -webkit-box-direction: normal;
        -webkit-flex-direction: column;
        -ms-flex-direction: column;
        flex-direction: column;
        -webkit-box-pack: end;
        -webkit-justify-content: flex-end;
        -ms-flex-pack: end;
        justify-content: flex-end;
        padding: 16px;
    }

    .demo-navigation {
        -webkit-box-flex: 1;
        -webkit-flex-grow: 1;
        -ms-flex-positive: 1;
        flex-grow: 1;
    }

    .demo-layout .demo-navigation .mdl-navigation__link {
        display: -webkit-box !important;
        display: -webkit-flex !important;
        display: -ms-flexbox !important;
        display: flex !important;
        -webkit-box-orient: horizontal;
        -webkit-box-direction: normal;
        -webkit-flex-direction: row;
        -ms-flex-direction: row;
        flex-direction: row;
```

```css
    -webkit-box-align: center;
    -webkit-align-items: center;
    -ms-flex-align: center;
    align-items: center;
    font-weight: 500;
}

.demo-navigation .mdl-navigation__link .material-icons {
    font-size: 24px;
    color: rgba(255, 255, 255, 0.56);
    margin-right: 32px;
}

.demo-content {
    max-width: 1080px;
}

.demo-card-wide.mdl-card {
    width: 512px;
    min-height: auto !important;
    margin: 16px;
}

.demo-card-wide > .mdl-card__title {
    color: #fff;
    background: #263238;
}

.demo-card-wide > .mdl-card__menu {
    color: #fff;
}

.react {
    position: absolute;
    top: 0;
    left: 0;
    width: 100%;
    height: 100%;
}

.mdl-layout__content {
    overflow: visible !important;
    position: relative;
    z-index: 10 !important;
```

```
    }

    .mdl-button--fab {
        position: fixed;
        bottom: 16px;
        right: 16px;
        z-index: 10 !important;
    }
```

These styles are mostly taken from the **Dashboard** layout files, though I've deleted styles that we don't need. Take a note of how the `.react` container element is stretched to the bounds of the window.

 Ideally, we would like to isolate the styles for each component inside each component. This can be achieved in a number of ways (which we briefly looked at in the previous chapter). Try to pull the styles for each of these components into the components themselves. It may be a bit more difficult to do if most of the styles come from the packaged MDL source files.

Let's take a look at the `Nav` component:

```
import React from "react";
import ReactDOM from "react-dom";

export default (props) => {
    var drawerClassNames = [
        "demo-drawer",
        "mdl-layout__drawer",
        "mdl-color--blue-grey-900",
        "mdl-color-text--blue-grey-50"
    ].join(" ");

    var navClassNames = [
        "demo-navigation",
        "mdl-navigation",
        "mdl-color--blue-grey-800"
    ].join(" ");

    var iconClassNames = [
        "mdl-color-text--blue-grey-400",
        "material-icons"
    ].join(" ");
```

```
var buttonIconClassNames = [
    "mdl-color-text--blue-grey-400",
    "material-icons"
].join(" ");

return (
    <div className={drawerClassNames}>
        <header className="demo-drawer-header">
            <img src="images/user.jpg"
                className="demo-avatar" />
        </header>
        <nav className={navClassNames}>
            <a className="mdl-navigation__link"
                href="/examples/login.html">
                <i className={buttonIconClassNames}
                    role="presentation">
                    lock
                </i>
                Login
            </a>
            <a className="mdl-navigation__link"
                href="/examples/page-admin.html">
                <i className={buttonIconClassNames}
                    role="presentation">
                    pages
                </i>
                Pages
            </a>
        </nav>
    </div>
);
};
```

This new `Nav` component is vastly different from the other React components we've created so far. For a start, it has no internal state, rendering only static content. It's not a class, but rather a plain arrow function. Since React 0.14, it has become possible to pass a function to the `ReactDOM.render`, whether directly or indirectly.

> You may also want to move the class arrays outside of the functions that use them, since they're not likely to change often. This isolates them away from the moving parts of each component and reduces the amount of work done each time the components are rendered.
>
> For the sake of simplicity, I've left them inside the render function, but you're welcome to move them as you extend or customize your components.

This style is far simpler to follow when it comes to stateless components. It's a pattern that we'll repeat as time goes on, so be on the lookout for it!

Then, we need to create the Login component:

```
import React from "react";
import ReactDOM from "react-dom";

export default (props) => {
    var contentClassNames = [
        "mdl-layout__content",
        "mdl-color--grey-100"
    ].join(" ");

    var gridClassNames = [
        "mdl-grid",
        "demo-content"
    ].join(" ");

    var fieldClassNames = [
        "mdl-textfield",
        "mdl-js-textfield"
    ].join(" ");

    return <div className={contentClassNames}>
        <form className={gridClassNames}>
            <div className={fieldClassNames}>
                <input className="mdl-textfield__input"
                    type="text" />
                <label className="mdl-textfield__label"
                    htmlFor="sample1">
                    Email...
                </label>
            </div>
            <div className={fieldClassNames}>
                <input className="mdl-textfield__input"
                    type="text" />
                <label className="mdl-textfield__label"
                    htmlFor="sample1">
                    Password...
                </label>
            </div>
        </form>
    </div>;
};
```

As you can see, input elements work the same as usual, with the addition of a few special MDL classes.

This gives us a pleasant login page:

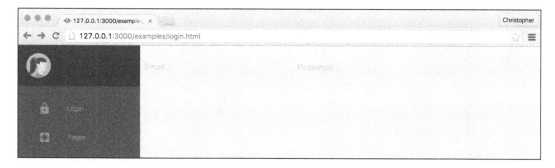

Updating page admin

We need to apply similar changes to the now-separate `page-admin.html` and `page-admin.js` files. Let's begin with the HTML:

```
<!DOCTYPE html>
<html>
    <head>
        <script src="/node_modules/babel-core/browser.js"></script>
        <script src="/node_modules/systemjs/dist/system.js"></script>
        <script src="https://storage.googleapis.com/code.getmdl.io/1.0.6/material.min.js"></script>
        <link rel="stylesheet" href="https://storage.googleapis.com/code.getmdl.io/1.0.6/material.indigo-pink.min.css" />
        <link rel="stylesheet" href="https://fonts.googleapis.com/icon?family=Material+Icons">
        <link rel="stylesheet" href="example.css" />
    </head>
    <body class="
        mdl-demo
        mdl-color--grey-100
        mdl-color-text--grey-700
        mdl-base">
        <div class="react"></div>
        <script>
            System.config({
                "transpiler": "babel",
                "map": {
                    "react": "/examples/react/react",
```

```
                    "react-dom": "/examples/react/react-dom"
                },
                "baseURL": "../",
                "defaultJSExtensions": true
            });

            System.import("examples/page-admin");
        </script>
    </body>
</html>
```

This is almost exactly the same as `login.html`, except that we load a different bootstrap file in this page. There are significant differences in `page-admin.js` though:

```
import React from "react";
import ReactDOM from "react-dom";
import Nav from "src/nav";
import Backend from "src/backend";
import PageAdmin from "src/page-admin";

var backend = new Backend();

var layoutClassNames = [
    "demo-layout",
    "mdl-layout",
    "mdl-js-layout",
    "mdl-layout--fixed-drawer"
].join(" ");

ReactDOM.render(
    <div className={layoutClassNames}>
        <Nav />
        <PageAdmin backend={backend} />
    </div>,
    document.querySelector(".react")
);
```

We still load in the `mdl-` classes and HTML structure, but we also include the same `Backend` bootstrapping as we included earlier. The `PageAdmin` component `render` method looks very different now:

```
render() {
    var contentClassNames = [
        "mdl-layout__content",
        "mdl-color--grey-100"
```

```
    ].join(" ");

    var addButtonClassNames = [
        "mdl-button",
        "mdl-js-button",
        "mdl-button--fab",
        "mdl-js-ripple-effect",
        "mdl-button--colored"
    ].join(" ");

    return (
        <div className={contentClassNames}>
            <button onClick={this.onInsert}
                className={addButtonClassNames}>
                <i className="material-icons">add</i>
            </button>
            {this.state.pages.map((page) => {
                return (
                    <Page {...page}
                        key={page.id}
                        onUpdate={this.onUpdate}
                        onDelete={this.onDelete} />
                );
            })}
        </div>
    );
}
```

Finally, we need to update the `PageView` component:

```
render() {
    var cardClassNames = [
        "demo-card-wide",
        "mdl-card",
        "mdl-shadow--2dp"
    ].join(" ");

    var buttonClassNames = [
        "mdl-button",
        "mdl-button--icon",
        "mdl-js-button",
        "mdl-js-ripple-effect"
    ].join(" ");

    return (
        <div className={cardClassNames}>
            <div className="mdl-card__title">
```

```
            <h2 className="mdl-card__title-text">
                {this.props.title}
            </h2>
        </div>
        <div className="mdl-card__supporting-text">
            {this.props.body}
        </div>
        <div className="mdl-card__menu">
            <button className={buttonClassNames}
                onClick={this.props.onEdit}>
                <i className="material-icons">edit</i>
            </button>
            <button className={buttonClassNames}
                onClick={this.props.onDelete}>
                <i className="material-icons">delete</i>
            </button>
        </div>
    </div>;
}
```

These changes don't do anything significant to the functionality we had previously, other than the CSS and HTML changes. We still create pages in exactly the same way. Also, we still edit and delete them in exactly the same way. We simply apply new visuals to an already functional interface.

The page admin section should now look like this:

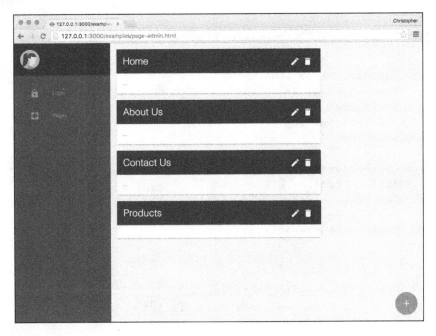

It's much better than before! One thing to note is that we haven't yet styled the `PageEdit` component, so consider that an exercise for next time.

> Pay careful attention to the example code files. A lot has changed since the last chapter, including splitting the example files and loading everything differently with SystemJS. You cannot continue on from the last chapter's code without making these changes and expect the examples in this chapter to work out of the box.

Alternative resources

Before we wrap up, I want to share a few resources that you might find helpful.

Font Squirrel

In this chapter, we used Roboto. More accurately, The MDL instructions told us how to embed a link to Roboto on Google Webfonts. If you would prefer to use your own custom fonts, then you may need to convert them.

You can convert font files at Font Squirrel:

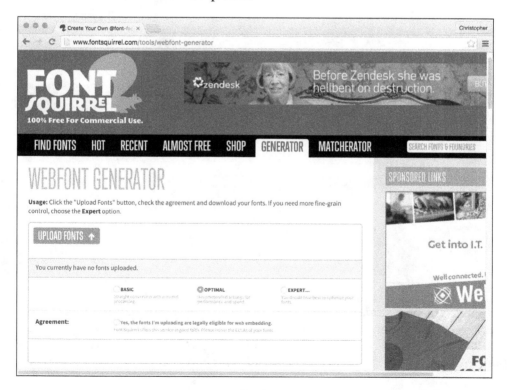

Head over to `http://www.fontsquirrel.com/tools/webfont-generator` and upload your font files. You'll start to download the converted files with helpful CSS files to get you started. We don't have time to cover all the intricacies of custom fonts, but the example files you download should set you on the right path.

Material UI

We created a bit of a mash-up between the MDL CSS/JavaScript and React. This might not always work or be as elegant as you would like. In such instances, check out `http://www.material-ui.com`.

Material UI has a huge range of components to choose from, as we can see in the following screenshot:

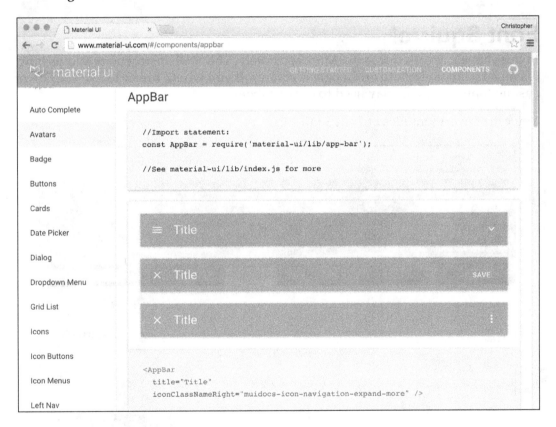

It's a catalogue of material design components built to work on top of React. We may use some of them in our CMS, but I'll make sure that I explain when we do. It's worth taking a look through the components it has to offer and deciding whether you'd prefer the purer approach of material design over the code we have so far.

Summary

In this chapter, we blasted through some of the concepts in material design. You learned to think of it as an ever-changing language that we must learn over time. We implemented a global navigation component using a new form of React component (a function). We also implemented a login page, which is in need of a server-side validation, and we made our `PageAdmin` component look heaps better!

In the next chapter, we'll look at how to change views without page reloads and some of the neat things we can do to make that experience beautiful.

6
Changing Views

In the previous chapter, we covered a bit about material design, and as a result, we split the login and page admin sections into different files. We stopped short of making the login redirect us to the page admin section.

In this chapter, you will learn how to change sections without reloading the page. We'll use this knowledge to create public pages for the website our CMS is meant to control.

We'll see how to work with the browser's address bar and location history. We'll also learn how to use popular libraries to abstract these things for us, so we can save time on writing boilerplate and concentrate on making our interfaces great!

Location, location, location!

Before we can learn about alternatives to reloading pages, let's take a look at how the browser manages reloads.

You've probably encountered the `window` object. It's a global catch-all object for browser-based functionality and state. It's also the default `this` scope in any HTML page:

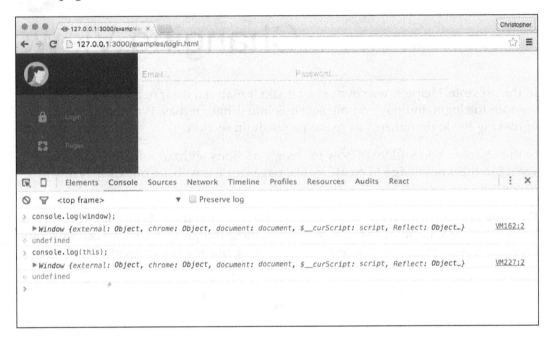

We've even accessed `window` earlier. When we rendered to `document.body` or used `document.querySelector`, these properties and methods were called on the `window` object. It's the same as calling `window.document.querySelector`.

Most of the time, `document` is the only property we need. That doesn't mean it's the only property useful to us. Try the following in the console:

```
console.log(window.location);
```

You should see something similar to the following:

```
Location {
    hash: ""
    host: "127.0.0.1:3000"
    hostname: "127.0.0.1"
    href: "http://127.0.0.1:3000/examples/login.html"
```

```
        origin: "http://127.0.0.1:3000"
        pathname: "/examples/login.html"
        port: "3000"
        ...
    }
```

If we were trying to work out which components to show based on the browser URL, this would be an excellent place to start. Not only can we read from this object, but we can also write to it:

```
<script>
    window.location.href = "http://material-ui.com";
</script>
```

Putting this in an HTML page or entering that line of JavaScript in the console will redirect the browser to www.material-ui.com. It's the same as clicking on a link to that website. And, if it's redirected to a different page (than the one the browser is pointing at), then it will cause a full page reload.

A bit of history

So how does this help us? We're trying to avoid full page reloads, after all. Let's experiment with this object.

Let's see what happens when we add something like #page-admin to the URL.

Adding #page-admin to the URL leads to the window.location.hash property being populated with the same. What's more, changing the hash value won't reload the page! It's the same as clicking on a link that had a hash in the href attribute. We can modify it without causing full page reloads, and each modification will store a new entry in the browser history.

Using this trick, we can step through a number of different states without reloading the page, and we will be able to backtrack each with the browser's back button.

Using browser history

Let's put this trick to use in our CMS. First, let's add a couple of functions to our Nav component:

```
export default (props) => {
    // ...define class names

    var redirect = (event, section) => {
        window.location.hash = `#${section}`;
        event.preventDefault();
    }

    return <div className={drawerClassNames}>
        <header className="demo-drawer-header">
            <img src="images/user.jpg"
                className="demo-avatar" />
        </header>
        <nav className={navClassNames}>
            <a className="mdl-navigation__link"
                href="/examples/login.html"
                onClick={(e) => redirect(e, "login")}>
                <i className={buttonIconClassNames}
                    role="presentation">
                    lock
                </i>
                Login
            </a>
            <a className="mdl-navigation__link"
                href="/examples/page-admin.html"
                onClick={(e) => redirect(e, "page-admin")}>
                <i className={buttonIconClassNames}
                    role="presentation">
                    pages
                </i>
```

```
                     Pages
                  </a>
               </nav>
            </div>;
    };
```

We add an `onClick` attribute to our navigation links. We created a special function that will change `window.location.hash` and prevent the default full page reload behavior the links would otherwise have caused.

> This is a neat use of the arrow functions, but we're ultimately creating three new functions in each render call. Remember that this can be expensive, so it's best to move the function creation out of render. We'll replace this shortly.

It's also interesting to see template strings in action. Instead of `"#" + section`, we can use `'#${section}'` to interpolate the section name. It's not as useful in small strings, but becomes increasingly useful in large ones.

Clicking on the navigation links will now change the URL hash. We can add to this behavior by rendering different components when the navigation links are clicked on:

```
import React from "react";
import ReactDOM from "react-dom";
import Component from "src/component";
import Login from "src/login";
import Backend from "src/backend";
import PageAdmin from "src/page-admin";

class Nav extends Component {
    render() {
        // ...define class names

        return <div className={drawerClassNames}>
            <header className="demo-drawer-header">
                <img src="images/user.jpg"
                    className="demo-avatar" />
            </header>
            <nav className={navClassNames}>
                <a className="mdl-navigation__link"
                    href="/examples/login.html"
                    onClick={(e) => this.redirect(e, "login")}>
                    <i className={buttonIconClassNames}
                        role="presentation">
```

```
                          lock
                    </i>
                    Login
              </a>
              <a className="mdl-navigation__link"
                 href="/examples/page-admin.html"
                 onClick={(e) => this.redirect(e, "page-admin")}>
                  <i className={buttonIconClassNames}
                     role="presentation">
                     pages
                  </i>
                  Pages
              </a>
          </nav>
      </div>;
}


redirect(event, section) {
    window.location.hash = '#${section}';

    var component = null;

    switch (section) {
        case "login":
            component = <Login />;
            break;
        case "page-admin":
            var backend = new Backend();
            component = <PageAdmin backend={backend} />;
            break;
    }

    var layoutClassNames = [
        "demo-layout",
        "mdl-layout",
        "mdl-js-layout",
        "mdl-layout--fixed-drawer"
    ].join(" ");

    ReactDOM.render(
        <div className={layoutClassNames}>
            <Nav />
            {component}
        </div>,
```

```
            document.querySelector(".react")
        );

        event.preventDefault();
    }
};
```

```
export default Nav;
```

We've had to convert the `Nav` function to a `Nav` class. We want to create the redirect method outside of render (as that is more efficient) and also isolate the choice of which component to render.

Using a class also gives us a way to name and reference the `Nav` component, so we can create a new instance to overwrite it from within the `redirect` method. It's not ideal to package this kind of code within a component, so we'll clean that up in a bit.

We can now switch between different sections without full page reloads.

There is one problem still to solve. When we use the browser's back button, the components don't change to reflect the component that should be shown for each hash. We can solve this in a couple of ways. The first approach we can try is checking the hash frequently:

```
componentDidMount() {
    var hash = window.location.hash;

    setInterval(() => {
        if (hash !== window.location.hash) {
            hash = window.location.hash;
            this.redirect(null, hash.slice(1), true);
        }
    }, 100);
}

redirect(event, section, respondingToHashChange = false) {
    if (!respondingToHashChange) {
        window.location.hash = `#${section}`;
    }

    var component = null;

    switch (section) {
        case "login":
            component = <Login />;
```

```
            break;
        case "page-admin":
            var backend = new Backend();
            component = <PageAdmin backend={backend} />;
            break;
    }

    var layoutClassNames = [
        "demo-layout",
        "mdl-layout",
        "mdl-js-layout",
        "mdl-layout--fixed-drawer"
    ].join(" ");

    ReactDOM.render(
        <div className={layoutClassNames}>
            <Nav />
            {component}
        </div>,
        document.querySelector(".react")
    );

    if (event) {
        event.preventDefault();
    }
}
```

Our `redirect` method has an extra parameter, to apply the new hash whenever we're not responding to a hash change. We also wrapped the call to `event.preventDefault` in case we don't have a click event to work with. Other than these changes, the `redirect` method is the same.

We also added a `componentDidMount` method in which we make a call to `setInterval`. We stored the initial `window.location.hash` property and checked 10 times a second to see whether it has changed. The hash value is `#login` or `#page-admin`, so we sliced the first character off and passed the rest to the `redirect` method.

Try clicking on the different navigation links and then using the browser's back button.

The second option is to use the newish `pushState` and `popState` methods on the `window.history` object. They're not very well supported yet, so you need to be careful when you handle older browsers, or ensure that you don't need to handle them.

You can learn more about `pushState` and `popState` at `https://developer.mozilla.org/en-US/docs/Web/API/History_API`.

There's an easier way to respond to users clicking links: the `hashchange` event. Instead of adding the `onClick` events to each of the links (and calling the `redirect` function every time), we can listen for the `hashchange` events and change to the appropriate view. There's a great tutorial on this at `https://medium.com/@tarkus/react-js-routing-from-scratch-246f962ededf`.

Using a router

Our hash code is functional but invasive. We shouldn't call the `render` method from inside a component (at least not the one we own). So, we will instead use a popular router to manage this stuff for us.

Download the router with the following command:

```
$ npm install react-router --save
```

Then, we need to put `login.html` and `page-admin.html` back into the same file:

```html
<!DOCTYPE html>
<html>
    <head>
        <script src="/node_modules/babel-core/browser.js"></script>
        <script src="/node_modules/systemjs/dist/system.js"></script>
        <script src="https://storage.googleapis.com/code.getmdl.io/1.0.6/material.min.js"></script>
        <link rel="stylesheet" href="https://storage.googleapis.com/code.getmdl.io/1.0.6/material.indigo-pink.min.css" />
        <link rel="stylesheet" href="https://fonts.googleapis.com/icon?family=Material+Icons" />
        <link rel="stylesheet" href="admin.css" />
    </head>
    <body class="
        mdl-demo
        mdl-color--grey-100
        mdl-color-text--grey-700
        mdl-base">
        <div class="react"></div>
        <script>
            System.config({
                "transpiler": "babel",
```

```
                    "map": {
                        "react": "/examples/react/react",
                        "react-dom": "/examples/react/react-dom",
                        "router": "/node_modules/react-router/umd/
ReactRouter"
                    },
                    "baseURL": "../",
                    "defaultJSExtensions": true
                });

            System.import("examples/admin");
        </script>
    </body>
</html>
```

Notice how we've added the `ReactRouter` file to the import map? We'll use that in `admin.js`. First, let's define our `layout` component:

```
import React from "react";
import ReactDOM from "react-dom";
import Component from "src/component";
import Nav from "src/nav";
import Login from "src/login";
import Backend from "src/backend";
import PageAdmin from "src/page-admin";
import {Router, browserHistory, IndexRoute, Route} from "router";

var App = function(props) {
    var layoutClassNames = [
        "demo-layout",
        "mdl-layout",
        "mdl-js-layout",
        "mdl-layout--fixed-drawer"
    ].join(" ");

    return (
        <div className={layoutClassNames}>
            <Nav />
            {props.children}
        </div>
    );
};
```

This creates the page layout we've been using and allows a dynamic content component. Every React component has a `this.props.children` property (or `props.children` in the case of a `function` component), which is an array of nested components. For example, consider the following component:

```
<App>
    <Login />
</App>
```

Inside the `App` component, `this.props.children` will contain a single item: an instance of the `Login`. Next, we'll define handler components for the two sections we want to route:

```
var LoginHandler = function() {
    return <Login />;
};


var PageAdminHandler = function() {
    var backend = new Backend();
    return <PageAdmin backend={backend} />;
};
```

We don't really need to wrap `Login` in `LoginHandler`, but I chose to do it to be consistent with `PageAdminHandler`. `PageAdmin` expects an instance of `Backend`, so we have to wrap it, as we see in this example.

Now, we can define routes for our CMS:

```
ReactDOM.render(
    <Router history={browserHistory}>
        <Route path="/" component={App}>
            <IndexRoute component={LoginHandler} />
            <Route path="login" component={LoginHandler} />
            <Route path="page-admin" component={PageAdminHandler} />
        </Route>
    </Router>,
    document.querySelector(".react")
);
```

There's a single root route for the path `/`. It creates an instance of `App`, so we always get the same layout. Then, we nest a `"login"` route and a `"page-admin"` route. These create instances of their respective components. We also define `IndexRoute` so that the login page will be displayed as a landing page.

We need to remove our custom history code from `Nav`:

```
import React from "react";
import ReactDOM from "react-dom";
import { Link } from "router";

export default (props) => {
    // ...define class names

    return <div className={drawerClassNames}>
        <header className="demo-drawer-header">
            <img src="images/user.jpg"
                className="demo-avatar" />
        </header>
        <nav className={navClassNames}>
            <Link className="mdl-navigation__link" to="login">
                <i className={buttonIconClassNames}
                    role="presentation">
                     lock
                </i>
                Login
            </Link>
            <Link className="mdl-navigation__link" to="page-admin">
                <i className={buttonIconClassNames}
                    role="presentation">
                     pages
                </i>
                Pages
            </Link>
        </nav>
    </div>;
};
```

Also, since we no longer need a separate `redirect` method, we can convert the class back into a statement component (`function`).

Note that we swapped anchor components for a new `Link` component. This interacts with the router to show the correct section when we click on the navigation links. We can also change the route paths without the need to update this component (unless we also change the route names).

In the preceding chapter, we split index.html into login.html and page-admin.html to see both sections just by changing the URL. In this chapter, we joined them back together, since we have a router to switch between them. You'll need to make the same changes or use the example code for this chapter in order for the examples to work.

Creating public pages

Now that we can easily switch between CMS sections, we can use the same trick to show the public pages of our website. Let's create a new HTML page just for these:

```html
<!DOCTYPE html>
<html>
    <head>
        <script src="/node_modules/babel-core/browser.js"></script>
        <script src="/node_modules/systemjs/dist/system.js"></script>
    </head>
    <body>
        <div class="react"></div>
        <script>
            System.config({
                "transpiler": "babel",
                "map": {
                    "react": "/examples/react/react",
                    "react-dom": "/examples/react/react-dom",
                    "router": "/node_modules/react-router/umd/
ReactRouter"
                },
                "baseURL": "..//",
                "defaultJSExtensions": true
            });

            System.import("examples/index");
        </script>
    </body>
</html>
```

This is a reduced form of admin.html without the material design resources. I think we can ignore the appearance of these pages for the moment while we focus on the navigation.

The public pages are stateless, so we can use the `function` components for them. Let's begin with the layout component:

```
var App = function(props) {
    return (
        <div className="layout">
            <Nav pages={props.route.backend.all()} />
            {props.children}
        </div>
    );
};
```

This is similar to the `App` admin component, but it also has a reference to `Backend`. We then define it when we render the components:

```
var backend = new Backend();

ReactDOM.render(
    <Router history={browserHistory}>
        <Route path="/" component={App} backend={backend}>
            <IndexRoute component={StaticPage} backend={backend} />
            <Route path="pages/:page" component={StaticPage}
backend={backend} />
        </Route>
    </Router>,
    document.querySelector(".react")
);
```

For this to work, we also need to define `StaticPage`:

```
var StaticPage = function(props) {
    var id = props.params.page || 1;
    var backend = props.route.backend;

    var pages = backend.all().filter(
        (page) => {
            return page.id == id;
        }
    );

    if (pages.length < 1) {
        return <div>not found</div>;
    }

    return (
        <div className="page">
```

```
        <h1>{pages[0].title}</h1>
        {pages[0].content}
      </div>
    );
  };
```

This component is more interesting. We access the `params` property, which is a map of all the URL path parameters defined for this route. We have `:page` in the path (`pages/:page`), so when we go to `pages/1`, the `params` object is `{"page":1}`.

We also pass `Backend` to `Page`, so we can fetch all pages and filter them by `page.id`. If no `page.id` is provided, we default to `1`.

After filtering, we check whether there are any pages. If not, we return a simple **Not found** message. Otherwise, we render the content of the first page in the array (since we expect the array to have a length of at least 1).

We now have a page for the public pages of the website:

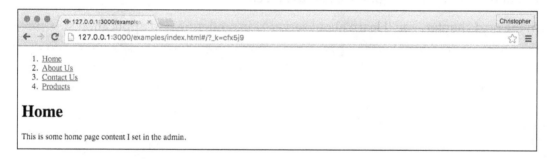

We can also add the `onEnter` and `onLeave` callbacks to each of our routes:

```
<Route path="pages/:page"
    component={StaticPage}
    backend={backend}
    onEnter={props => console.log("entering")}
    onLeave={() => console.log("leaving")} />
```

As the current route changes, the previous route will trigger `onLeave`, as will each parent component up the inheritance chain. Once all the `onLeave` callbacks are triggered, the router will begin to trigger the `onEnter` callbacks down the inheritance chain. We didn't really use inheritance much (owing to how simple our navigation is), but it's still important to remember that `onLeave` is triggered before `onEnter`.

This is useful if we want to commit any unsaved data to our backend, log the progress of a user through the interface or anything else that might depend on the user navigating between pages on the site.

In addition to this, we want to animate different pages as they are rendered. We can combine them with `React.addons.CSSTransitionGroup`, which we saw in *Chapter 4, Styling and Animating Components*. As new components are rendered inside the `App` component, we will be able to animate them in exactly the same way. Just include `div.layout` in a `React.addons.CSSTransitionGroup` component and you should be all set!

Summary

In this chapter, you learned about how the browser stores URL history, and how we can manipulate it to load different sections without full page reloads. It introduced a bit of complexity, but we also saw that there are other alternatives (for example, the `hashchange` event) that reduce the complexity while still reducing the number of full page reloads we need to perform.

You also learned about a popular React router and used it to abstract the manual location tracking or changing we had to do before.

In the next chapter, you'll learn about server-side rendering and application structure.

7
Rendering on the Server

In the last chapter, you learned how to render different sections of our CMS without reloading the page. We even created a way to see the public pages of our website, using the same routing techniques.

So far, we did everything in the browser. We stored pages in local storage. We used the website and CMS as if they were hosted on the Internet, but we're the only ones who can see it. If we want to share our creations with others, we need some kind of server-side technology.

In this chapter, we will take a brief look at some aspects of server-side JavaScript and React programming. We'll see how React works outside of the browser, and how we can persist and share data with many people in real-time.

Rendering components to strings

One of the beautiful things about React is that it works in many places. It is aimed at rendering interfaces efficiently, but those interfaces can extend outside of the DOM and the browser.

You can use React to render native mobile interfaces (https://facebook.github.io/react-native), or even plain HTML strings. This becomes useful when we want to reuse the component code in different places.

We can, for instance, build an intricate data table component for our CMS. We can ship that component to an iPad application or even render it from the web server as a way of minimizing page load time.

It's the latter example that we will try in this chapter. To begin, we need to install the source versions of React and React DOM libraries:

```
$ npm install --save babel-cli babel-preset-react babel-preset-es2015
react react-dom
```

We've already seen examples of the React libraries, but these new ones (from BabelJS) will give us a way of using ES6 and JSX on the server. They even provide an alternative to running our code directly through Node.js. Normally, we would run server-side JavaScript code using the following command:

```
$ node server.js
```

But, we can now use a BabelJS version, as follows:

```
$ node_modules/.bin/babel-node server.js
```

We need to tell BabelJS which code presets to apply to our code. By default, it will apply a select few ES6 transformations, but not all of them. It also won't handle JSX, unless we load that preset as well. We do this by creating a file called `.babelrc`:

```
{
    "presets": ["react", "es2015"]
}
```

We're used to seeing ES6 `import` statements, but perhaps not the RequireJS `require` statements. These are similar in function, and Node.js uses them as a means of importing code from external scripts.

We also require a file called `hello-world.js`:

```
var React = require("react");
var ReactDOMServer = require("react-dom/server");

console.log(
    ReactDOMServer.renderToString(<div>hello world</div>)
);
```

There's something new again! We have loaded a new React library, called `ReactDOMServer` and render a string from a `div` component. Usually we would use something like `React.render(component, element)` in the browser. But, here we're only interested in the HTML string the component generates. Consider running the following:

```
$ babel-node examples/server.js
```

When we run the preceding command, we will see something resembling this:

```
<div data-reactid=".yt0g9w8kxs" data-react-checksum="-
1395650246">hello world</div>
```

Perhaps not exactly what we expect, but it looks like valid HTML. We can use this!

Creating a simple server

Now that we can render components to HTML strings, it would serve us better to have a way to respond to HTTP requests with HTML responses.

Fortunately, Node.js also includes a neat little HTTP server library. We can use the following code, in the `server.js` file, to respond to HTTP requests:

```
var http = require("http");

var server = http.createServer(
    function (request, response) {
        response.writeHead(200, {
            "Content-Type": "text/html"
        });

        response.end(
            require("./hello-world")
        );
    }
);


server.listen(3000, "127.0.0.1");
```

To use the HTTP server library, we need to require/import it. We create a new server, and in the callback parameter, respond to individual HTTP requests.

For each request, we set a content type and respond with the HTML value of our `hello-world.js` file. The server listens on port `3000`, which means you'll need to open `http://127.0.0.1:3000` to see this message.

Before we can do that, we also need to adjust `hello-world.js` slightly:

```
var React = require("react");
var ReactDOMServer = require("react-dom/server");

module.exports = ReactDOMServer.renderToString(
    <div>hello world</div>
);
```

The `module.exports = ...` statement is the RequireJS equivalent of the `export default ...` statement that we're used to seeing. The result is that this file will return the component HTML string whenever it is required by another.

If we open the URL (`http://127.0.0.1:3000`) in the browser, we should see a `hello world` message, and inspecting it will show similar React HTML for the component:

 You can learn more about the Node.js HTTP server at `https://nodejs.org/api/http.html`.

Creating a server backend

One of the things our CMS is still missing is public, persistent pages. So far, we stored them in local storage, and that's OK while we build up our CMS components. But a time will come when we would want to share our data with the world.

For this to work, we need some storage mechanism. Even if that storage is only in memory for as long as the server is running. Sure, we could use a relational database or an object store to persist our CMS pages. For now, let's keep things simple. An in-memory store (pages variable) should do for now.

So, how should we structure this data store? Whatever storage medium we choose, the interface will need to reach out to the server to store and retrieve data. There are two mainstream options I want to explore...

Communicating through Ajax requests

Ajax is a loaded word. For the purposes of this chapter, I want you to think of it only as a means to fetch data from a server and send data to it using HTTP requests.

We've just seen how we can respond to HTTP requests, so we're half-way there! At this point, we can inspect requests to determine the URL and method of each HTTP request. A browser may be requesting something like GET http://127.0.0.1:3000/pages to get all the pages. So, if the method matches POST and the path matches /pages, then we can respond with the appropriate pages.

Luckily for us, others have been down this path before. Projects such as ExpressJS have sprung up to provide some scaffolding for us. Let's install ExpressJS:

```
$ npm install --save express
```

Now, we can convert our simple HTTP server to be based on ExpressJS:

```
var app = require("express")();
var server = require("http").Server(app);

app.get("/", function (request, response) {
    response.send(
        require("./hello-world")
    );
});


server.listen(3000);
```

 Remember that you'll need to restart the node server.js command after each change to these JavaScript files.

This should render exactly the same in a browser. However, it's a lot easier to define application endpoints for new things:

```
app.get("/", function (request, response) {
    response.send(
        require("./hello-world")
    );
});

app.get("/pages", function (request, response) {
    response.send(
        JSON.stringify([ /* ... */ ])
    );
});
```

The JSON.stringify statement converts a JavaScript variable to a string representation, which is a useful format for communicating over a network.

We also have access to methods such as app.post for handling POST requests. It's really easy to start designing HTTP endpoints for our backend data.

Then, in the browser, we need a way to make these requests. One common solution is to use a library such as jQuery. Sometimes that's a good idea, but usually only when you need more than just the Ajax functionality jQuery provides.

If you're looking for a lean solution, try something such as SuperAgent (https://github.com/visionmedia/superagent) or even the new Fetch API (https://developer.mozilla.org/en/docs/Web/API/Fetch_API):

```
var options = {
    "method": "GET"
};

fetch("http://127.0.0.1/pages", options).then(
    function(response) {
        console.log(response);
    }
);
```

Using this approach, we can slowly replace the local storage parts of our backend with calls to the server. There, we can store page data in an array, a relational database, or an object store.

Ajax is a time-tested approach to communicate between the browser and the server. It's a well-supported technique with many kinds of shims for older browsers (from iframes to flash).

 You can learn more about ExpressJS at http://expressjs.com.

Communicating through web sockets

Sometimes, it's better to have fast, bi-directional communication between the browser and the server.

At such a time, you can try web sockets. They're an upgrade to the traditional HTTP communication seen in Ajax. To work with them easily, we need the help of Socket.IO:

```
npm install --save socket.io
```

Now we can access a new object, which we'll call `io`:

```
// ...enable JSX/ES6 compilation

var app = require("express")();
var server = require("http").Server(app);
var io = require("socket.io")(server);

app.get("/", function (request, response) {
    response.send(
        require("./hello-world")
    );
});

// ...define other endpoints

io.on("connection", function (socket) {
    console.log("connection");

    socket.on("message", function (message) {
        console.log("message: " + message);

        io.emit("message", message);
    });
});

server.listen(3000);
```

 The "message" can be anything. You can send messages of different types simply by changing this to something else. If you send a message with "chat message" or "page command", then you need to add event listeners for the same message type.

We create a new `io` instance with a reference to the HTTP server. Web socket connections begin with an HTTP request, so that's a good place to listen for them.

When new web socket connections are made, we can start to listen for messages. For now, we can just send the messages back. Socket.IO provides the web socket client script, but we do still need to connect and send messages. Let's update `hello-world.js`:

```
var React = require("react");
var ReactDOMServer = require("react-dom/server");

var script = {
    "__html": `
        var socket = io();

        socket.on("message", function (message) {
            console.log(message);
        });

        socket.emit("message", "hello world");
    `
};

module.exports = ReactDOMServer.renderToString(
    <div>
        <script src="/socket.io/socket.io.js"></script>
        <script dangerouslySetInnerHTML={script}></script>
    </div>
);
```

There are two important things to note in this block of code:

- We can use multiline strings as part of the ES6 syntax. Instead of single or double quotes, we can use backticks for strings that we want to span over multiple lines.

- We can set the innerHTML (which is something we need to do to get JavaScript to render on the browser through this HTTP response) via the `dangerouslySetInnerHTML` attribute.

 You can learn more about `dangerouslySetInnerHTML` at `https://facebook.github.io/react/tips/dangerously-set-inner-html.html`.

In our web socket examples, the flow of data resembles the following:

1. An HTTP and web socket server listen on `http://127.0.0.1:3000`.
2. Requests to / return some browser scripts.
3. These scripts begin a connection request to the server.
4. The server picks up these connection requests and adds event listeners for new messages after the connections are successfully opened.
5. The browser scripts add event listeners for new messages and immediately a send message to the server.
6. The server's event listeners are triggered and the messages are re-sent to all open sockets.
7. The browser's event listeners are triggered and the messages are written to the console.

> In this example, we broadcast the messages (from the server) to all open sockets. You can limit the messages to specific socket connections using something such as `socket.emit("message", message)`. Check the Socket.IO documentation for examples.

You should see the `hello world` message in the console:

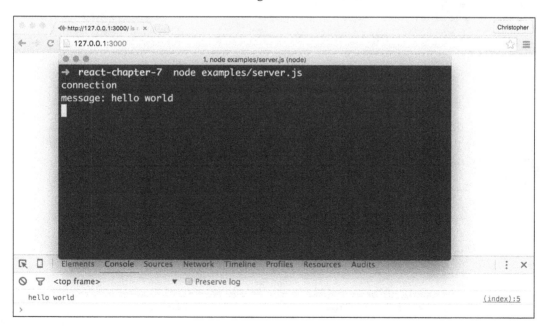

You can learn more about Socket.IO at `http://socket.io`.

Structuring server-side applications

When it comes to HTTP and web socket servers, it's usually a good idea to separate the endpoint code from the server initialization code. Some folks like to create separate routes files, which can then be required by the `server.js` file. Still others like to have each endpoint as a separate file and define routes as glue between `server.js` and these "handler" files.

Perhaps that's enough for the kinds of applications you will build, or perhaps you like a more prescriptive structure to your applications, something such as AdonisJS (`http://adonisjs.com`), for example.

Adonis is a beautifully structured MVC framework for Node.js applications. It uses many cool tricks (such as generators) to enable a clean API for defining templates, request handlers, and database code.

A typical request can be handled in the following way:

```
class HomeController {
    * indexAction (request, response) {
        response.send("hello world");
    }
}

module.exports = HomeController
```

You would define this class in a file called `app/Http/Controllers/HomeController.js`. To have this file rendered, when browsers go to the home page of your website, you can define a route in `app/Http/routes.js`:

```
const Route = use("Route");

Route.get("/", "HomeController.indexAction");
```

You can couple this with some persistent, relational database storage:

```
const Database = use("Database");

const users = yield Database.table("users").select("*");
```

All in all, AdonisJS provides a lot of structure to an otherwise open and interpretive landscape. It reminds me a lot of the popular PHP framework — Laravel, which itself draws queues from the popular Ruby on Rails framework.

 You can learn more about AdonisJS at `http://adonisjs.com`.

Summary

In this chapter, you learned how to render components on the server. We created a simple HTTP server and then upgraded it to allow multiple endpoints and web sockets. Finally, we looked briefly at how we can structure our server-side code and quickly looked at the AdonisJS MVC framework.

In the next chapter, you will learn about some popular React design patterns that you can apply to your components and interfaces.

8
React Design Patterns

In the last chapter, we looked at React on the server. We created a simple HTTP server followed by multiple endpoints and web sockets.

In this chapter, we will take a step back and consider the component architecture we have built so far. We'll look at a couple of popular React design patterns and how we can make subtle improvements to our architecture.

Where we are

Let's take a look at the things we have created so far and how they interact with each other. If you've been following closely, this may all be familiar to you; but stick with it.

We will talk about how these interactions are failing us and how we can improve them. From the moment our interface begins to render, we start to see the following things happen:

1. We begin by creating a backend object. We use this as a store for the pages in our application. This has methods such as `add`, `edit`, `delete`, and `all`. It also acts as an event emitter, notifying listeners whenever pages change.

2. We create a `PageAdmin` React component and pass the `Backend` object to it. The `PageAdmin` component uses the `Backend` object as a data source for other page components, all of which are created within the `PageAdmin` render method. The `PageAdmin` component listens for changes in `Backend` as soon as it is mounted. It stops listening after it is unmounted.

3. The `PageAdmin` component has a few callbacks, which it passes down to the other page components it creates. These provide a way for child components to trigger changes in the `Backend` object.

4. Through user interaction, components such as `PageEditor` and `PageView` trigger the callback functions they receive from `PageAdmin`. These then trigger changes in the `Backend` object.

5. Data changes in `Backend`. At the same time, `Backend` notifies event listeners that the data has changed and `PageAdmin` is one of those listeners.

6. The `PageAdmin` component updates its internal state to the newest version of the `Backend` pages, which causes other page components to re-render.

We can imagine this as follows:

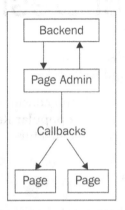

We can even reduce our existing code to the essential parts of this architecture. Let's re-implement listing and adding pages without styles or the build chain. We can use this as a starting point for the architectural improvements later in this chapter. This will also be a good place to recap some of the new ES6 features we've seen so far and learn about a few new ones.

I don't want to repeat the whole build chain here, but we do need some help to use ES6 and JSX in our code:

```
$ npm install --save babel-cli babel-preset-react
babel-preset-es2015 eventemitter3 react react-dom
```

We enable ES6/JSX transformers in `.babelrc`:

```
{
    "presets": ["react", "es2015"]
}
```

We can run this code with the following command:

```
$ node_modules/.bin/babel-node index.js
```

This will transform the ES6/JSX code in `index.js` and all the files it imports.

We began with the src/backend.js file:

```js
import Emitter from "eventemitter3";

class Backend extends Emitter {
    constructor() {
        super();

        this.id = 1;
        this.pages = [];
    }

    add() {
        const id = this.id++;
        const title = `New Page ${id}`;

        const page = {
            id,
            title
        };

        this.pages.push(page);
        this.emit("onAdd", page);
    }

    getAll() {
        return this.pages;
    }
}

export default Backend;
```

Backend is a class with internal id and pages properties. The id property acts as an auto-increment identity value for each new page object. It has the add and getAll methods, which add new pages and return all pages, respectively.

In ES6, we can define constants (variables which cannot be changed after they are defined and assigned). These are great for when we only need to define a variable once, as they guard against unintended changes.

We assign the next identity value and increment the internal id property so that the next identity value will be different. ES6 template strings allow us to interpolate variables (like we do with the identity value) and define multiline strings.

We can define objects with keys matching defined local variable names using the new ES6 object literal syntax. In other words, { title } means the same as { title: title }.

Each time a new page is added, Backend emits its onAdd event to any listeners. We can see all of this in action with the following code (in index.js):

```
import Backend from "./src/backend";

let backend = new Backend();

backend.on("onAdd", (page) => {
    console.log("new page: ", page);
});

console.log("all pages: ", backend.getAll());

backend.add();
console.log("all pages: ", backend.getAll());
```

In ES6, the let keyword works similarly to var. The difference is that var is scoped to the enclosing function, where let is scoped to the enclosing block:

```
function printPages(pages) {
    for (var i = 0; i < pages.length; i++) {
        console.log(pages[i]);
    }

    // i == pages.length - 1

    for (let j = 0; j < pages.length; j++) {
        console.log(pages[j]);
    }

    // j == undefined
}
```

If you run this Backend code, you should see the following output:

```
all pages:  []
new page:  { id: 1, title: 'New Page 1' }
all pages:  [ { id: 1, title: 'New Page 1' } ]
```

We can combine this with the `PageAdmin` component (in `src/page-admin.js`):

```
import React from "react";

const PageAdmin = (props) => {
    return (
        <div>
            <a href="#"
                onClick={(e) => {
                    e.preventDefault();
                    props.backend.add();
                }}>
                add page
            </a>
            <ol>
                {props.backend.all().map((page) => {
                    return (
                        <li key={page.id}>
                            {page.title}
                        </li>
                    );
                })}
            </ol>
        </div>
    );
};

export default PageAdmin;
```

This is a stateless function version of our previous `PageAdmin` component. We can use it with the following code (in `index.js`):

```
import Backend from "./src/backend";
import PageAdmin from "./src/page-admin";
import React from "react";
import ReactDOMServer from "react-dom/server";

let backend = new Backend();

backend.add();
backend.add();
backend.add();
```

```
console.log(
    ReactDOMServer.renderToString(
        <PageAdmin backend={backend} />
    )
);
```

This will generate the following output:

```
<div data-reactid=".51gm9pfn5s" data-react-checksum="865425333">
    <a href="#" data-reactid=".51gm9pfn5s.0">add page</a>
    <ol data-reactid=".51gm9pfn5s.1">
        <li data-reactid=".51gm9pfn5s.1.$1">New Page 1</li>
        <li data-reactid=".51gm9pfn5s.1.$2">New Page 2</li>
        <li data-reactid=".51gm9pfn5s.1.$3">New Page 3</li>
    </ol>
</div>
```

Now, if we were rendering this into an HTML page, we would click on the **add page** link and a new page would be added to the list of existing pages inside `Backend`. We also created `PageAdmin` as a class so that we could add an event listener in the `componentWillMount` life cycle method. This listener would then update the child `Page` components with an updated array of pages.

The `PageAdmin` component was used to render the `Page` components, which in turn rendered the `PageView` and `PageEditor` components to show and edit pages, respectively. We passed callback functions down through each layer so that every component could trigger changes in the `Backend` object without knowing how it stores or manipulates the data.

Flux

At this stage, we encounter the first design pattern (and the improvements we can make). Flux is a pattern proposed by Facebook that defines the flow of data in an interface.

 Flux is not a library, but Facebook has released a few tools that help implement the design pattern. You don't have to use those tools to implement Flux. To install it, run `npm install --save flux` in addition to the previous dependencies.

We implemented something very close to Flux, but our implementation is at a slight disadvantage. Our `Backend` class does too much. We call it directly to add and fetch pages. It emits events when new pages are added. It's tightly coupled with the components that use it.

So, we'd have a hard time replacing it with a new `Backend` class (unless the methods, events and return values were in the exact same format). We'd have a hard time using multiple data backends. We don't even really have unidirectional flow of data because we send *and* receive data from `Backend`.

Flux differs here; it defines separate objects for *making changes* and *getting data*. Our `Backend` class becomes a *dispatcher* for the former and a *store* for the latter. What's more, instructions to change application state take the form of message objects (called *actions*).

We can imagine this as follows:

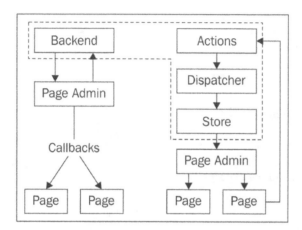

 These code examples will require another library, which you can install with `npm install --save flux`.

We can implement this design change by creating a new `PageDispatcher` object (in `src/page-dispatcher.js`):

```
import { Dispatcher } from "flux";

const pageDispatcher = new Dispatcher();

export default pageDispatcher;
```

The `Dispatcher` class isn't too complex. It has a couple of methods, which we will use shortly. What's important to note is that we are exporting an instance of the `Dispatcher` class, not a subclass. We only need one dispatcher for our page operations. So, we use it as a kind of singleton, even though we've not coded it specifically to be a singleton.

If you're unfamiliar with the singleton pattern, you can learn about it at https://en.wikipedia.org/wiki/Singleton_pattern. The basic idea is that we create a class for something (or, in this case, use an existing class) but we only ever create and use a single instance of the class.

The second part of this change is a class called `PageStore`, which we create in `src/page-store.js`:

```
import Emitter from "eventemitter3";
import PageDispatcher from "./page-dispatcher";

class PageStore extends Emitter {
    constructor() {
        super();

        this.id = 1;
        this.pages = [];
    }

    add() {
        // ...add new page
    }

    getAll() {
        return this.pages;
    }
}

const pageStore = new PageStore();

PageDispatcher.register((payload) => {
    if (payload.action === "ADD_PAGE") {
        pageStore.add();
    }

    pageStore.emit("change");
});

export default pageStore;
```

This class closely resembles the `Backend` class. One notable change is that we no longer emit the `onAdd` event after adding new pages. Instead, we register a sort of event listener on `PageDispatcher`, which is how we know to add new pages to `PageStore`. It's possible to call `PageStore.add` directly, but here, we do that in response to actions being dispatched to `PageDispatcher`. This is how those actions look (in `src/index.js`):

```
import PageAdmin from "./src/page-admin";
import PageDispatcher from "./src/page-dispatcher";
import PageStore from "./src/page-store";

PageStore.on("change", () => {
    console.log("on change: ", PageStore.getAll());
});

console.log("all pages: ", PageStore.getAll());

PageDispatcher.dispatch({
    "action": "ADD_PAGE"
});

console.log("all pages: ", PageStore.getAll());
```

 Dispatchers trigger event listeners in all registered stores. If you dispatch an action through a dispatcher, all stores will be notified, no matter the payload.

Now, stores don't only manage collections of objects (like our pages). They're not an application database. They're meant to store all application states. Perhaps we should change a few methods to make this clearer, beginning in `src/page-store.js`:

```
class PageStore extends Emitter {
    constructor() {
        super();

        this.id = 1;
        this.pages = [];
    }

    handle(payload) {
        if (payload.action == "ADD_PAGE") {
            // ...add new page
        }
    }
}
```

```
        getState() {
            return {
                "pages": this.pages
            };
        }
    }

    const pageStore = new PageStore();

    PageDispatcher.register((payload) => {
        if (payload.action === "ADD_PAGE") {
            pageStore.handle(payload);
        }

        pageStore.emit("change");
    });
```

We're still calling this store `PageStore`, but it can hold many other kinds of state besides an array of pages. It could, for instance, store filter and sorting state as well. For each new action, we would just need to add some code to the `handle` method.

We also need to adjust the calling code in `index.js`:

```
    PageStore.on("change", () => {
        console.log("change: ", PageStore.getState());
    });

    console.log("all state: ", PageStore.getState());

    PageDispatcher.dispatch({
        "action": "ADD_PAGE"
    });

    console.log("all state: ", PageStore.getState());
```

When we run this, we should see the following output:

```
    all state:  { pages: [] }
    change:  { pages: [ { id: 1, title: 'New Page 1' } ] }
    all state:  { pages: [ { id: 1, title: 'New Page 1' } ] }
```

Now, we need to implement these changes in `src/page-admin.js`:

```
    import React from "react";
    import PageDispatcher from "./page-dispatcher";
    import PageStore from "./page-store";
```

```
class PageAdmin extends React.Component {
    constructor() {
        super();
        this.state = PageStore.getState();
        this.onChange = this.onChange.bind(this);
    }
    componentDidMount() {
        PageStore.on("change", this.onChange);
    }
    componentWillUnmount() {
        PageStore.removeListener("change", this.onChange);
    }
    onChange() {
        this.setState(PageStore.getState());
    }
    render() {
        return (
            <div>
                <a href="#"
                    onClick={(e) => {
                        e.preventDefault();

                        PageDispatcher.dispatch({
                            "action": "ADD_PAGE"
                        });
                    }}>
                    add page
                </a>
                <ol>
                    {this.state.pages.map((page) => {
                        return (
                            <li key={page.id}>
                                {page.title}
                            </li>
                        );
                    })}
                </ol>
            </div>
        );
    }
};

export default PageAdmin;
```

Finally, we can update `index.js` to reflect these new changes:

```
import PageAdmin from "./src/page-admin";
import PageDispatcher from "./src/page-dispatcher";
import PageStore from "./src/page-store";
import React from "react";
import ReactDOMServer from "react-dom/server";

PageDispatcher.dispatch({
    "action": "ADD_PAGE"
});

// ...dispatch the same thing a few more times

console.log(
    ReactDOMServer.renderToString(
        <PageAdmin />
    )
);
```

If we run this code, we see very similar output to the code we had before implementing Flux.

Benefits of using Flux

In a sense, we're still tightly coupling the code that renders interface elements and the code that stores and manipulates state. We've just created a bit of a barrier between them. So, what do we gain from this approach?

To start with, Flux is a popular design pattern for React applications. We can talk about actions, dispatchers, and stores and be sure that other React developers will know exactly what we mean. This decreases the learning curve for bringing new developers into React projects.

We've also separated state storage from user and system actions. We have a single, universal object through which we can send actions. These may result in changes to multiple stores, which in turn can trigger changes in multiple parts of our interface. We don't need of multiple stores in our simple example, but complex interfaces can benefit from multiple stores. In these cases, a single dispatcher and multiple stores work well together.

It's worth noting that while we've named the Flux dispatcher in such a way that we could have more than one dispatcher, apps usually only have one. It's also common to have the data backend and dispatcher act as singletons. I've chosen to deviate from this based on how we began our application and how we're going to end it.

Redux

Flux leads us to separate our `Backend` class into a dispatcher and a store as a means of decoupling from a single state store and implementation. This leads to quite a bit of boilerplate, and we still have some coupling (to global dispatcher and store objects). It's great to have some terminology to work with, but it doesn't feel like the best solution.

What if we could decouple actions and storage and remove the global objects? This is what Redux seeks to do along with reducing boilerplate code and bringing about better standards overall.

 You can download the Redux tools by running `npm install --save redux react-redux` in addition to the previous dependences. Redux is also just a pattern, but the tools in these libraries will help greatly in setting things up.

Redux can be a lot to take in at first, but there are some simple underlying things which bind it all together. For a start, there's the idea that all state is held in immutable objects. This state should only be transformed by pure functions, which take in the current state, and produce a new state. These pure functions are also sometimes called idempotent, which means they can be run many times (with the same input) and produce the exact same output every time. Let's explore this idea with some code in `index.js`:

```
const transform = (state, action) => {
    let id = 1;
    let pages = state.pages;

    if (action.type == "ADD_PAGE") {
        pages = [
            ...state.pages,
            {
                "title": "New Page " + id,
                "id": id++
            }
```

```
        ];
    }

    return {
        pages
    };
};

console.log(
    transform({ "pages": [] }, { "type": "ADD_PAGE" })
);
```

Here, we have a function that takes an initial state value and modifies it in the presence of the same sort of action we created for Flux. This is a pure function with no side-effects. A new state object is returned, and we even use the ES6 spread operator as a way of concatenating the pages into a new array. It's really the same as doing the following:

```
pages = pages.concat({
    "title": "New Page " + id,
    "id": id++
});
```

When we prefix an array with . . ., its values expand as if we wrote them all out in a row. This transformer function is called a *reducer,* named after the reduce part of *MapReduce* (https://en.wikipedia.org/wiki/MapReduce). That is, Redux defines reducers as a way of reducing an initial state by passing it through one or more reducers to a new state.

We give this reducer to a store similar to the one we created for Flux:

```
import { createStore } from "redux";

const transform = (state = { "pages": [] }, action) => {
    // ...create a new state object, with a new page
};

const store = createStore(transform);

store.dispatch({ "type": "ADD_PAGE" });

console.log(
    store.getState()
);
```

The store also acts as a dispatcher, so this is much closer to our original code. We register listeners on the store, so we can be notified of changes to state. We can use a `PageAdmin` component similar to the one we make for Flux (in `src/page-admin.js`):

```
import React from "react";

class PageAdmin extends React.Component {
    constructor(props) {
        super(props);
        this.state = this.props.store.getState();
        this.onChange = this.onChange.bind(this);
    }
    componentDidMount() {
        this.removeListener =
            this.props.store.register(this.onChange);
    }
    componentWillUnmount() {
        this.removeListener();
    }
    onChange() {
        this.setState(this.props.store.getState());
    }
    render() {
        return (
            <div>
                <a href="#"
                    onClick={(e) => {
                        e.preventDefault();

                        this.props.store.dispatch({
                            "type": "ADD_PAGE"
                        });
                    }}>
                    add page
                </a>
                <ol>
                    {this.state.pages.map((page) => {
                        // ...render each page
                    })}
                </ol>
            </div>
        );
    }
};

export default PageAdmin;
```

Also, we can render all of this with a few small changes to index.js:

```js
import { createStore } from "redux";
import PageAdmin from "./src/page-admin";
import React from "react";
import ReactDOMServer from "react-dom/server";

const transform = (state = { "pages": [] }, action) => {
    let id = 1;
    let pages = state.pages;

    if (action.type == "ADD_PAGE") {
        pages = [
            ...state.pages,
            {
                "title": "New Page " + id,
                "id": id++
            }
        ];
    }

    return {
        pages
    };
};

const store = createStore(transform);

store.dispatch({ "type": "ADD_PAGE" });

console.log(
    ReactDOMServer.renderToString(
        <PageAdmin store={store} />
    )
);
```

We can imagine a Redux application like this:

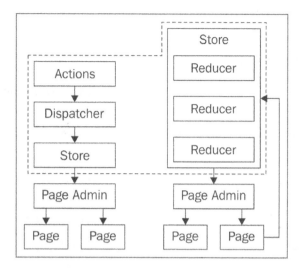

So, we've removed the global dependencies. We've almost come full-circle—from our original code to Flux to Redux.

Using context

As you build increasingly complex components, you may discover a frustrating side-effect to all this. In Redux, the store acts as a dispatcher. So, if you want to dispatch from components deep within a component hierarchy, you need to pass the store through multiple components that may not even need it themselves.

Consider, for a moment, building our CMS interface components to dispatch actions directly to the store. We may arrive at a hierarchy similar to this:

```
React.render(
    <PageAdmin store={store}>
        {store.getState().pages.map((page) => {
            <Page key={page.id} store={store}>
                <PageView {...page} store={store} />
                <PageEditor {...page} store={store} />
            </Page>
        })}
    </PageAdmin>
    document.querySelector(".react")
);
```

Those nested components could also be part of a render method.

It becomes tiresome passing these stores down to each component level in the interface. Fortunately, there is a solution to this problem. It's called *context*, and it works like this. First, we create a new component and modify how things are rendered in index.js:

```
class Provider extends React.Component {
    getChildContext() {
        return {
            "store": this.props.store
        };
    }
    render() {
        return this.props.children;
    }
}

Provider.childContextTypes = {
    "store": React.PropTypes.object
};

console.log(
    ReactDOMServer.renderToString(
        <Provider store={store}>
            <PageAdmin />
        </Provider>
    )
);
```

The new component is called Provider, and it renders all nested components without modification. However, it does define a new life cycle method called getChildContext. This returns an object with the property values that we want nested components to be given. These values are similar to props; however, they are implicitly provided to nested components.

Along with getChildContext, we also need to define Provider.childContextTypes. These React.PropTypes should match what we want to return from getChildContext. Similarly, we need to modify PageAdmin:

```
class PageAdmin extends React.Component {
    constructor(props, context) {
```

```
                super(props, context);
                this.state = context.store.getState();
                this.onChange = this.onChange.bind(this);
            }
            componentDidMount() {
                this.removeListener =
                    this.context.store.register(this.onChange);
            }
            componentWillUnmount() {
                this.removeListener();
            }
            onChange() {
                this.setState(this.context.store.getState());
            }
            render() {
                return (
                    <div>
                        <a href="#"
                            onClick={(e) => {
                                e.preventDefault();

                                this.context.store.dispatch({
                                    "type": "ADD_PAGE"
                                });
                            }}>
                            add page
                        </a>
                        <ol>
                            {this.state.pages.map((page) => {
                                // ...render each page
                            })}
                        </ol>
                    </div>
                );
            }
        };


    PageAdmin.contextTypes = {
        "store": React.PropTypes.object
    };
```

When we define PageAdmin.contextTypes, we allow components higher up in the
hierarchy to provide their context to PageAdmin. In this case, context will contain a
reference to the store. To that end, we change props.store to context.store.

This is a common occurrence in Redux architecture. It is so common that such a `Provider` component comes standard with the Redux tools. We can replace our `Provider` implementation with the one imported from *ReactRedux*:

```
import { Provider } from "react-redux";

console.log(
    ReactDOMServer.renderToString(
        <Provider store={store}>
            <PageAdmin />
        </Provider>
    )
);
```

We don't even need to define `Provider.childContextTypes`. We do, however, still need to define `PageAdmin.contextTypes` to opt in to the provided context though.

Benefits of Redux

Redux is growing in popularity, and it's no surprise. It has all the benefits of Flux (such as true unidirectional flow of data and less coupling to a single backend implementation) without all of the boilerplate. There's much more to learn about it, but what we've covered will set you in great stead to begin architecting better applications!

> You can learn more about Redux at `https://egghead.io/series/getting-started-with-redux`. It's a fantastic video course by the creator of Redux.

Summary

In this chapter, you learned about modern architectural design patterns that we can use to build better React applications. We began with the Flux pattern and moved on to Redux.

In the next chapter, we will look at how to create plugin-based components to allow our interfaces to be extended by others.

Thinking of Plugins

9

In the previous chapter, we looked at a couple of design patterns that we could use to build our applications. There are reasons for and against the use of Flux and Redux, but they generally improve the structure of React applications.

A good structure is essential for any large-scale application. Cobbling things together may work for small experiments, but design patterns are an integral part of maintaining anything larger. They do not say much in the way of creating extendable components, though. In this chapter, we're going to look at a few ways that we can use to make our components extendable by replacing them, injecting functionality, and composing interfaces from dynamic lists of components.

We're going to review a few related software design concepts and take a look at how they can assist us (and others) when we want to replace parts of our application with modified components and alternative implementations.

Dependency injection and service location

Dependency injection and *service location* are interesting concepts that are not limited to React development. To really understand them, let's move away from components for a while. For a moment, imagine that we wanted to create a sitemap. To do this, we could perhaps use code resembling the following code:

```
let backend = {
    getAll() {
        // ...return pages
    }
};
```

```
class SitemapFormatter {
    format(items) {
        // ...generate xml from items
    }
}
function createSitemap() {
    const pages = backend.getAll();
    const formatter = new SitemapFormatter();

    return formatter.format(
        pages.filter(page => page.isPublic)
    );
}

let sitemap = createSitemap();
```

In this example, createSitemap has two dependencies. Firstly, we fetch pages from backend. This is a kind of global storage object. We used something similar to this when we looked at the Flux architecture.

The second dependency is to the SitemapFormatter implementation. We use it to take a list of pages and return some kind of markup, summarizing these pages in the list. We're hardcoding both of these dependencies in a way that is okay in small doses, but they are problematic as the application expands.

For instance, what if we wanted to use this sitemap generator with multiple backends? What if we also wanted to try alternative implementations of the formatter? Right now, we've coupled the sitemap generator to a single backend and a single formatter implementation.

Dependency injection and service location are two possible solutions to this problem.

Dependency injection

We've already used dependency injection, in subtle ways. This looks like the following:

```
function createSitemap(backend, formatter) {
    const pages = backend.getAll();

    return formatter.format(
        pages.filter(page => page.isPublic)
    );
}

let formatter = new SitemapFormatter();
let sitemap = createSitemap(backend, formatter);
```

Dependency injection is all about moving dependencies out of the functions and classes that use them. This is not about avoiding their use; but rather it is creating new instances outside and passing them in through function parameters.

There are two kinds of dependency injection: constructor injection and setter injection. This may illustrate the difference:

```
class SitemapGenerator {
    constructor(formatter) {
        this._formatter = formatter;
    }

    set formatter(formatter) {
        this._formatter = formatter;
    }
}

let generator = new SitemapGenerator(new SitemapFormatter());

generator.formatter = new AlternativeSitemapFormatter();
```

We can inject dependencies through the constructor and assign them to properties, or we can create setters for them. We saw constructor injection a few times already, but setter injection is another valid means of injecting dependencies. We could also use normal functions to inject dependencies, but then we wouldn't be able to set or get them through object properties.

Similarly, when we define component properties, we're essentially injecting these property values as constructor dependencies.

Factories and service locators

An alternative solution would be to encapsulate the logic to create new instances and use references to this factory-like object when looking for dependencies:

```
class Factory {
    createNewFormatter() {
        // ...create new formatter instance
    }

    getSharedBackend() {
        // ...get shared backend instance
    }
}
```

```
const factory = new Factory();

const formatter = factory.createNewFormatter();
const backend = factory.getSharedBackend();
```

We can then pass around an instance of the `Factory` class, or even inject this as a dependency. In other dynamic languages, such as PHP, this has become a common practice. We can then use these factories to create new instances that are based on some initial criteria. We can have a factory to create new database connections and connect to MySQL or SQLite, which is based on a connection type that we specify.

An alternative would be to create a number of objects and store them inside a common service locator object:

```
let locator = new ServiceLocator();
locator.set("formatter", new Formatter());
locator.set("backend", new Backend());
```

Likewise, we can inject the locator as a dependency and fetch the actual dependencies, as needed:

```
class SitemapGenerator {
    constructor(locator) {
        this.formatter = locator.get("formatter");
        this.backend = locator.get("backend");
    }
}

let generator = new SitemapGenerator(locator);
```

Fold

Fortunately, we do not need to build and maintain factories, dependency injectors, and service locators. There are already many to choose from, especially in JavaScript. We will discuss one in particular. Remember when we discussed rendering React components on the server? We looked at an MVC application framework, called AdonisJS.

The creator of AdonisJS also maintains a dependency injection container, called *Fold*. Some of the things that Fold does is interesting, and we want to share them with you.

We can install Fold using the following command:

```
$ npm install --save adonis-fold
```

In previous chapters, we created a workflow to run ES6 code through Node.js. We recommend that you re-create this setup for some of the code in this chapter.

We can then start to use it to register and resolve objects:

```
import { Ioc } from "adonis-fold";

Ioc.bind("App/Authenticator", function() {
    // ...return a new authenticator object
});

let authenticator = Ioc.use("App/Authenticator");
```

 Fold introduces a global use function, so we could use it without needing to import Ioc each time.

We use `bind` to assign an alias to a factory-like function. When this alias is *used*, this factory function will be called and the result returned. This becomes even more powerful when we have large dependency graphs:

```
Ioc.bind("App/Authenticator", function() {
    const repository = Ioc.use("App/UserRepository");
    const crypto = Ioc.use("App/Crypto");

    return new Authenticator(repository, crypto);
});
```

We can compose calls to `bind` and `use`. In this example, creating a new App/Authenticator will in turn resolve App/UserRepository and App/Crypto from the container.

What's more is that we can use Fold to load class files automatically. So, let's suppose that we have an Authenticator class file resembling the following (in src/Authenticator.js):

```
class Authenticator {
    // ...do some authentication!
}

module.exports = Authenticator;
```

Usually we export classes or functions with export
default ...; but in this case, we're just assigning
the class to module.exports. This makes it easier
for Fold to do more interesting things with our code.

We can autoload this with the following code:

```
Ioc.autoload("App", __dirname + "/src");

const Authenticator = Ioc.use("App/Authenticator");

let authenticator = new Authenticator();
```

We can also use regular classes as singletons with a slightly different binding syntax:

```
Ioc.singleton("App/Backend", function() {
    // ...this will only be run once!
    return new Backend();
});
```

 The use works in the same way, whether you use bind
or singleton.

Fold really shines when it comes to resolving dependencies recursively. Let's change
Authenticator:

```
class Authenticator {
    static get inject() {
        return ["App/Repository", "App/Crypto"];
    }

    constructor(repository, crypto) {
        this.repository = repository;
        this.crypto = crypto;
    }
}

module.exports = Authenticator;
```

We can use getters (a feature of ES6) to overload property access for a static `inject` property. This just means that a function will be run whenever we write `Authenticator.inject`. Fold uses this static array property to work out which dependencies to resolve. Therefore, we can create `Repository` (in `src/Repository.js`), as follows:

```
class Repository {
    // ...probably fetches users from a data source
}

module.exports = Repository;
```

We can also create `Crypto` (in `src/Crypto.js`), as follows:

```
class Crypto {
    // ...probably performs cryptographic comparisons
}

module.exports = Crypto;
```

The function of these classes isn't important. What is important is how Fold connects them together:

```
Ioc.autoload("App", __dirname + "/src");

let authenticator = Ioc.make("App/Authenticator");
```

The first line creates a link between the `App/` class prefix and the class files that we want to load. Therefore, a class in `src/Foo/Bar.js` will be loaded when we create `App/Foo/Bar`. Similarly, aliases defined in the static inject array property will be connected to their relevant constructor parameters when we use `Ioc.make`.

Why this matters

If we inject dependencies, we can easily replace one part of an application with another because dependencies aren't named within the classes that depend on them. These classes aren't responsible for creating new instances, only receiving instances created on the outside.

If we use a service locator (especially one that resolves dependencies recursively), we can avoid a lot of boilerplate during a bootstrapping phase.

What do we gain from being able to replace parts of our application?

We allow other developers to inject behavior into our application by replacing core parts of the application. Imagine we have the following `Authenticator` method:

```
class Authenticator {
    static get inject() {
        return ["App/Repository", "App/Crypto"];
    }

    constructor(repository, crypto) {
        this.repository = repository;
        this.crypto = crypto;
    }

    authenticate(email, password) {
        // ...authenticate the user details
    }
}
```

Now imagine that we want to add logging to all authentication. We can change the `Authenticator` class directly. This is easy if we *own* the code, but we often use third-party libraries. We can create a decorator (in `src/AuthenticatorLogger.js`):

```
class AuthenticatorLogger {
    static get inject() {
        return ["App/Authenticator"];
    }

    constructor(authenticator) {
        this.authenticator = authenticator;
    }

    authenticate(email, password) {
        this.log("authentication attempted");
        return this.authenticator.authenticate(email, password);
    }

    log(message) {
        // ...store the log message
    }
}

module.exports = AuthenticatorLogger;
```

Decorators are classes that augment the functionality of other classes, usually by composing an instance of the class that they augment. You can learn more about this pattern at https://en.wikipedia.org/wiki/Decorator_pattern.

This new class expects an `Authenticator` dependency and adds transparent logging to the `authenticate` method. We can override the default (autoload) behavior by rebinding `App/Authenticator`:

```
const Authenticator = Ioc.use("App/Authenticator");
const AuthenticatorLogger = Ioc.use("App/AuthenticatorLogger");

Ioc.bind("App/Authenticator", function() {
    return new AuthenticatorLogger(Ioc.make(Authenticator));
});

let authenticator = Ioc.make("App/Authenticator");
```

Let's think about this in terms of components. Imagine that we have a list of pages that are presented to us by a `PagesComponent` component (in `src/Page.js`):

```
import React from "react";

class PagesComponent extends React.Component {
    constructor(props, context) {
        super(props, context);
        // ...get context.store state
    }
    componentDidMount() {
        // ...add context.store change listener
    }
    componentWillUnmount() {
        // ...remove context.store change listener
    }
    render() {
        // ...return a list of pages
        return <div>pages</div>;
    }
}

module.exports = PagesComponent;
```

We can autoload this using Fold, as follows:

```
import React from "react";
import ReactDOMServer from "react-dom/server";

const PagesComponent = Ioc.use("App/PagesComponent");

let rendered = ReactDOMServer.renderToString(
    <PagesComponent />
);
```

Now, imagine that another developer came along and wanted to add some extra chrome around the list of pages. They could dig into the node_modules folder and directly edit the component, but this would be messy. Instead (and as we're using a dependency injection container), they can override the alias to App/PagesComponent:

```
const PagesComponent = Ioc.use("App/PagesComponent");

Ioc.bind("App/PagesComponent{}", function() {
    return (
        <PagesComponent />
    );
});

// ...then, when we want to decorate the component

class PagesComponentChrome extends React.Component {
    render() {
        return (
            <div className="chrome">
                {this.props.children}
            </div>
        )
    }
}

Ioc.bind("App/PagesComponent{}", function() {
    return (
        <PagesComponentChrome>
            <PagesComponent />
        </PagesComponentChrome>
    );
});
```

```
// ...some time later

let rendered = ReactDOMServer.renderToString(
    Ioc.use("App/PagesComponent{}")
);
```

> Things get a bit tricky when it comes to the React.Component subclasses versus instances of these subclasses. The ReactDOM.render and ReactDOMServer.renderToString expect instances are created when we use <SomeComponent/> in JSX. This may be helpful to register both forms in the container: bindings for a class reference and bindings for factory functions that create instances of these classes. We've suffixed the latter with { }, which we can use directly in a render method.

It may be a little easier to understand this last part by making the following small change:

```
// ...some time later

const NewPagesComponent = Ioc.use("App/PagesComponent{}");

let rendered = ReactDOMServer.renderToString(
    <div>{NewPagesComponent}</div>
);
```

In this way, we allow other developers to replace parts of the application with custom classes or component decorators. There's definitely some work to be done in terms of creating a team standard for this pattern, but the basic idea is solid.

> You can learn more about Fold at http://adonisjs.com/docs/2.0/ioc-container.

Extending with callbacks

Another method to create more pluggable components is to expose (and act on) event callbacks. We saw something similar already, but let's take a look at this anyway. Suppose we have a PageEditorComponent class, as follows:

```
import React from "react";

class PageEditorComponent extends React.Component {
    onSave(e, refs) {
```

```
            this.props.onSave(e, refs);
        }
        onCancel(e, refs) {
            this.props.onCancel(e, refs);
        }
        render() {
            let refs = {};

            return (
                <div>
                    <input type="text"
                        ref={ref => refs.title = ref} />
                    <input type="text"
                        ref={ref => refs.body = ref} />
                    <button onClick={e => this.onSave(e, refs)}>
                        save
                    </button>
                    <button onClick={e => this.onCancel(e, refs)}>
                        cancel
                    </button>
                </div>
            );
        }
    }


    PageEditorComponent.propTypes = {
        "onSave": React.PropTypes.func.isRequired,
        "onCancel": React.PropTypes.func.isRequired
    };


    module.exports = PageEditorComponent;
```

 This is another bit of code that would run best through one of the workflows that we created earlier (that allow rendering components in the browser) or https://jsbin.com. We're interested in looking at some dynamic behavior, so it's important that we can click on things!

As we saw earlier, we can pass onSave and onCancel callbacks through properties from some higher component. Each React component can have a ref callback. A reference to the DOM node is passed to this callback, so we can use methods such as focus and properties such as value. This works well to synchronize state with a common backend or store. However, what can we do to add some custom validation?

We can add optional callback properties (and `propTypes`) and incorporate these in our `onSave` and `onCancel` methods:

```
class PageEditorComponent extends React.Component {
    onSave(e, refs) {
        if (this.props.onBeforeSave) {
            if (!this.props.onBeforeSave(e, refs)) {
                return;
            }
        }

        this.props.onSave(e, refs);

        if (this.props.onAfterSave) {
            this.props.onAfterSave(e, refs);
        }
    }
    onCancel(e, refs) {
        this.props.onCancel(e, refs);
    }
    render() {
        let refs = {};

        return (
            <div>
                <input type="text"
                    ref={ref => refs.title = ref} />
                <input type="text"
                    ref={ref => refs.body = ref} />
                <button onClick={e => this.onSave(e, refs)}>
                    save
                </button>
                <button onClick={e => this.onCancel(e, refs)}>
                    cancel
                </button>
            </div>
        );
    }
}

PageEditorComponent.propTypes = {
    "onSave": React.PropTypes.func.isRequired,
    "onCancel": React.PropTypes.func.isRequired,
    "onBeforeSave": React.PropTypes.func,
    "onAfterSave": React.PropTypes.func,
};
```

We can then define additional steps at key points in the component's behavior:

```
const onSave = (e, refs) => {
    // ...save the data
    console.log("saved");
};

const onCancel = (e, refs) => {
    // ...cancel the edit
    console.log("cancelled");
};

const onBeforeSave = (e, refs) => {
    if (refs.title.value == "a bad title") {
        console.log("validation failed");
        return false;
    }

    return true;
};

ReactDOM.render(
    <PageEditorComponent
        onBeforeSave={onBeforeSave}
        onSave={onSave}
        onCancel={onCancel} />,
    document.querySelector(".react")
);
```

The `onSave` method checks whether an optional `onBeforeSave` property is defined. If so, this callback is run. If the callback returns `false`, we can use this as a way to prevent the default component save behavior. We still need the default save or cancel behavior to work, so these properties are required. The others are optional but useful.

Stores, reducers, and components

Building on these concepts, the final thing that we want you to look at is how this all fits together inside a Redux architecture.

 If you've skipped ahead to this chapter, make sure that you have a firm understanding of Redux by reading the previous chapter.

Let's begin with a `PageComponent` class (for individual pages, in a list):

```
import React from "react";

class PageComponent extends React.Component {
    constructor(props) {
        super(props);
        this.state = props.store.getState();
    }
    componentDidMount() {
        this.remove = this.props.store.register(
            this.onChange
        );
    }
    componentWillUnmount() {
        this.remove();
    }
    onChange() {
        this.setState(this.props.store.getState());
    }
    render() {
        const DummyPageViewComponent = use(
            "App/DummyPageViewComponent"
        );

        const DummyPageEditorComponent = use(
            "App/DummyPageEditorComponent"
        );

        const DummyPageActionsComponent = use(
            "App/DummyPageActionsComponent"
        );

        return (
            <div>
                <DummyPageViewComponent />
                <DummyPageEditorComponent />
                <DummyPageActionsComponent />
            </div>
        );
    }
}

module.exports = PageComponent;
```

The Dummy*Component classes can be anything, really. We created a few "empty" components in the source code that goes with this chapter. The main thing is that PageComponent composes a few other components.

Nothing too fancy here: we compose a few components and hook into the usual Redux stuff. This is complemented by some new service location stuff:

```
import { combineReducers, createStore } from "redux";

Ioc.bind("App/Reducers", function() {
    return [
        (state = {}, action) => {
            let pages = state.pages || [];

            if (action.type == "UPDATE_TITLE") {
                pages = pages.map(page => {
                    if (page.id = payload.id) {
                        page.title = payload.title;
                    }

                    return page;
                });
            }

            return {
                pages
            };
        }
    ];
});

Ioc.bind("App/Store", function() {
    const reducers = combineReducers(
        Ioc.use("App/Reducers")
    );

    return createStore(reducers);
});

const Store = Ioc.use("App/Store");
const PageComponent = Ioc.use("App/PageComponent");
```

```
let rendered = ReactDOMServer.renderToString(
    <PageComponent store={Store} />
)
```

We're using a new `combineReducers` method, which takes an array of reducers and produces a new mega-reducer. Let's make the order and inclusion of the child components configurable:

```
render() {
    const components = [
        use("App/DummyPageViewComponent"),
        use("App/DummyPageEditorComponent"),
        use("App/DummyPageActionsComponent"),
    ];

    return (
        <div>
            {components.map((Component, i) => {
                return <Component key={i} />;
            })}
        </div>
    );
}
```

Two interesting things are happening here:

- In ES6, the `Array.prototype.map` method passes a second parameter to the callback. This is the numeric index for the current iteration of the array that is being mapped. We can use this as the `key` parameter when we're creating a list of child components.

- We can use dynamic component names. Pay careful attention to the capitalization of `Component`. If the component name variable starts with a lowercase letter, React will assume a literal value.

Now that we're building a dynamic list of components, we can move the default list out of this component:

```
Ioc.bind("App/PageComponentChildren", function() {
    return [
        use("App/DummyPageViewComponent"),
        use("App/DummyPageEditorComponent"),
        use("App/DummyPageActionsComponent"),
    ];
});
```

We can then replace this list in `PageComponent.render`:

```
render() {
    const components = use("App/PageComponentChildren");

    return (
        <div>
            {components.map((Component, i) => {
                return <Component key={i} />;
            })}
        </div>
    );
}
```

Building on what we learned earlier about Fold, we can override this list when we want to add plugins! We can include a plugin to e-mail a snapshot of a page to someone:

```
const PageComponentChildren = use("App/PageComponentChildren");

Ioc.bind("App/PageComponentChildren", function() {
    return [
        ...PageComponentChildren,
        use("App/DummyPageEmailPluginComponent"),
    ];
});

let extended = ReactDOMServer.renderToString(
    <PageComponent store={Store} />
);
```

This new plugin configuration can be miles away from the core definition of `PageComponent`, and we don't have to change any core code to make this work. We can add new reducers in exactly the same way (thereby altering our store or dispatcher behavior):

```
const Reducers = use("App/Reducers");

Ioc.bind("App/Reducers", function() {
    return [
        ...Reducers,
        (state, action) => {
            if (action.type == "EMAIL_PAGE") {
                // ...email the page
            }
```

```
            return state;
        }
    ]
});
```

In this way, other developers can create entirely new components and reducers and apply them effortlessly to the system that we've already built.

Summary

In this chapter, we looked at a few methods that we could use to make our components (and general architecture) open to extension without requiring core modification. There's a lot to take in here and not nearly enough community standardization for this to be the final word on pluggable components. Hopefully, there's enough here for you to design the right plugin architecture for your application.

In the next chapter, we will look at various ways to test the components and classes that we've built so far. We'll continue to see the benefits of things, such as dependency injection and service location, while also learning about a few new tools.

10
Testing Components

In the last chapter, we looked at ways of making our components friendly for plugin developers. We saw a few of the benefits of dependency injection and how AdonisJS Fold can help us achieve it with minimal effort.

In this chapter, we will learn about testing—automated testing, effective testing, before-you-make-a-mess-of-your-code testing. We will learn about the benefits of testing and the different kinds of tests.

Eat your vegetables

Is there something you really don't like to eat? Perhaps it's a kind of vegetable or fruit. When I was a kid, there were many things I didn't like to eat. I couldn't even remember what many of them tasted like, and they didn't hurt me. I just made up my mind that they were bad, and I didn't like them.

Some developers have similar habits. Are there things you don't like to do as a developer? Not because they're difficult or bad, but just because...

For me, testing was one of those things. I learned about testing many years after I started programming, and it's still something I need to actively work on. I know why it's good, and why the common arguments against testing are bad. Still, I need to convince myself to continually test my work well.

I had to learn that it's not enough just to click through an interface, that testing isn't really testing unless it can be run automatically, that testing isn't really useful unless it happens continuously, and that testing is often very useful as part of a design phase before any implementation happens.

Here are some reasons why I believe these things. Perhaps you'll find them useful as you learn about testing or even as you try to convince people why they should plan and budget for testing.

I can't stress enough on the importance of testing. The concepts we look at here are just the tip of the iceberg. If you really want to learn about testing and writing testable code, I highly recommend that you read *Clean Code* (by Robert C. Martin).

Design by testing

Testing can be a powerful design tool for code as much as wireframes can be for interactive interfaces. Sometimes, it's good to make a rapid prototype of the code you think can work for you. But once you know how you want your code to behave, it's useful to write some assertions for this behavior.

Put the prototype to one side and start creating a checklist of the behavior you now know your code should have. Perhaps this is a good time to involve the product owners, as you essentially create a contract of functionality you have yet to implement.

This kind of a testing-first approach is often referred to as **test-driven development** (**TDD**). Tests are useful whether or not you write them first. But if you do write them first, they can help you shape the behavior of your code at a critical stage of a project.

Documentation by testing

Unless you have a folder of examples or extensive documentation, tests may be the only way for you to demonstrate what your code is supposed to do and how it is supposed to do it.

You (or the developers who work with your code) may know little of what your code is supposed to do, but if you write good tests, they can learn interesting things about it. Tests can reveal the parameters of functions, the ways in which functions break, and even what code is unused.

Sleep by testing

Few things set me on edge quite like deploying critical code changes to large production systems. Does your team follow the "never deploy on a Friday" rule? If you had a good suite of tests, you could deploy fearlessly.

Tests are an excellent way to discover regressions in code. Want to know if a change you're making will affect other parts of the application? If the application is well tested, you'll know the moment it does.

In summary, a good test suite will help you keep your code doing what it should and let you know when you've broken it. Tests are great.

 Whether you write tests before or after the rest of your application code, having any tests is usually better than having no tests. You don't have to follow TDD principles, but they have been known to improve the design of code. And grown-ups know to try broccoli before dismissing it.

Types of tests

Many books can (and have been) filled with the intricacies of testing. There's a lot of jargon and we could go on for quite some time. Instead, I want to focus on a handful of terms, which I think will be most useful to us. There are two common kinds of tests we can write.

Unit tests

Unit tests are tests that focus on one small, practical unit of work at a time. Given a non-trivial class or component, a unit test will focus on just one method or even just a single part of that method (if the method does many things).

To illustrate this, consider the following example code:

```
class Page extends React.Component {
    render() {
        return (
            <div className="page">
                <h1>{this.props.title}</h1>
                {this.props.content}
            </div>
        );
    }
}

class Pages extends React.Component {
    render() {
        return (
            <div className="pages">
                {this.getPageComponents()}
            </div>
        );
    }
```

```
getPageComponents() {
    return this.props.pages.map((page, key) => {
        return this.getPageComponent(page, key);
    });
}

getPageComponent(page, key) {
    return (
        <li key={key}>
            <Page {...page} />
        </li>
    );
}
}

let pages = [
    {"title": "Home", "content": "A welcome message"},
    {"title": "Products", "content": "Some products"},
];

let component = <Pages pages={pages} />;
```

 In previous chapters, we created a workflow for being able to run the ES6 code through Node.js. I recommend that you recreate this setup for some of the code in this chapter, or use a site such as http://jsbin.com/.

A unit test for the Page component could be something like this: given an instance of this component, and an object with a title "Home" and content "A welcome message", when I call something such as ReactDOMServer.render, I see markup containing an h1 element with the same title and a few data-reactid attributes.

We test a small, practical unit of work. In this case, Page has a single method with a small focus. We can test the whole component at once, assured that we're testing something small and focused.

On the other hand, a unit test for Pages can be something like this: given an instance of this component with the pages property containing an array of well-formed page objects, when I call getPageComponents, the getPageComponent method is called once for each page object with the correct properties each time.

We would write separate tests for each method since they have different focuses and produce different results. We wouldn't test all of the pages together in a unit test.

Functional tests

As compared to unit tests, functional tests are less concerned with such a narrow focus. Functional tests still test more areas, but they don't require as much unit isolation as unit tests. We can test the whole `Pages` component in a single functional test, perhaps, as follows: given an instance of this component with the `pages` property containing an array of well-formed page objects, when I call something such as `ReactDOMServer.render`, I see markup containing all pages and their correct properties.

We can test a lot more in a shorter period of time using functional tests. The downside to this is that the causes of errors are harder to pinpoint. Unit tests immediately point to the causes of smaller errors, while functional tests often only show that the group of functionality isn't working as expected.

 All of this is to say — the more accurately and granularly you test your code, the easier it will be to pinpoint the causes of errors. You can write a single functional test or 20 unit tests for the same code. So you need to balance the available time with the importance of detailed testing.

Testing with assertions

Assertions are the spoken/written language constructs made in the code. They look and function similar to how I've been speaking about them. In fact, most tests are structured in the same way we've been describing tests:

- Given some pre-conditions
- When something happens
- We see some post-conditions

The first two points happen as we create objects and components and call their various methods. Assertions happen in the third point. Node.js ships with a few basic assertion methods, which we can use to write our first tests:

```
import assert from "assert";

assert(
    rendered.match(/<h1 data-reactid=".*">Home<\/h1>/g)
);
```

There are quite a few assertion methods we can use:

- `assert(condition)`, `assert.ok(condition)`
- `assert.equal(actual, expected)`
- `assert.notEqual(actual, expected)`
- `assert.strictEqual(actual, expected)`
- `assert.notStrictEqual(actual, expected)`
- `assert.deepEqual(actual, expected)...`
- `assert.notDeepStrictEqual(actual, expected)`
- `assert.throws(function, type)`

You can add an optional custom message string to the parameters for any of these methods. The custom message will be displayed in place of the default error messages for each of these.

We can write these quite simply—creating a `tests.js` file, importing classes and components, and making assertions against their methods and markup.

If you prefer a more expressive syntax, consider installing the `assertthat` library:

$ npm install --save-dev assertthat

You can then write tests similar to the following:

```
import assert from "assertthat";

assert.that(actual).is.equals.to(expected);
assert.that(actual).is.between(expectedLow, expectedHigh);
assert.that(actual).is.not.undefined();
```

The example code for this chapter includes tests that you can inspect and run. I've also created a BabelJS-powered way to use ES6 and JSX in the tests. You can run the tests with the following command:

$ npm test

This runs the NPM script defined as follows:

```
"scripts": {
  "test": "node_modules/.bin/babel-node index.js"
}
```

Don't be alarmed if you see nothing after running that. The tests are set up in such a way that you'll only see errors if the tests fail. If you see no errors, everything is OK!

Testing for immutability and idempotence

When we looked at Flux and Redux, one of the interesting things we saw is that they recommend immutable types and idempotent functionality (like in reducers). If we were to test for these qualities, we can! Let's install a helper library:

```
$ npm install --save-dev deep-freeze
```

Then, let's consider the following example:

```javascript
import { createStore } from "redux";

const defaultState = {
    "pages": [],
};

const reducer = (state = defaultState, action) => {
    if (action.type === "ADD_PAGE") {
        state.pages.push(action.payload);
    }

    return state;
};

let store = createStore(reducer);

store.dispatch({
    "type": "ADD_PAGE",
    "payload": {
        "title": "Home",
        "content": "A welcome message",
    },
});

let state = store.getState();

assert(
    state.pages.filter(page => page.title == "Home").length > 0
);
```

 If this is unfamiliar to you, refer back to the chapter on design patterns (*Chapter 8, React Design Patterns*).

Here, we have an example reducer, store, and assertion. The reducer handles a single action—adding new pages. When we dispatch an ADD_PAGE action to the store, the reducer adds a new page to the pages state array. This reducer is not idempotent—it cannot be run with the same input and always produce the same output.

We can see this by freezing the default state:

```
import freeze from "deep-freeze";

const defaultState = freeze({
    "pages": [],
});
```

When we run this, we should see an error such as Can't add property 0, object is not extensible. Remember that we can fix this problem by returning a new, modified state object from our reducer:

```
const reducer = (state = defaultState, action) => {
    if (action.type === "ADD_PAGE") {
        let pages = state.pages;

        pages = [
            ...pages,
            action.payload,
        ];
    }

    return {
        "pages": pages,
    };
};
```

Now, we can dispatch the same actions and always get the same results. We're no longer modifying the state in-place, but rather returning a new, modified state. The particulars of idempotence and immutability are better explained elsewhere; but the important thing to note is how we test for idempotence.

We can freeze the objects/arrays we want to remain idempotent and be assured that we're not modifying the things we don't want to modify.

Connecting to Travis

Having tests is a great first step toward better code, but it's also important to run them often. There are many ways to do this (such as Git hooks or build steps), but the way I prefer is to connect my projects to *Travis*.

Travis is a continuous integration service, meaning that Travis watches for changes in a GitHub repository (`https://github.com`) and triggers tests for those changes.

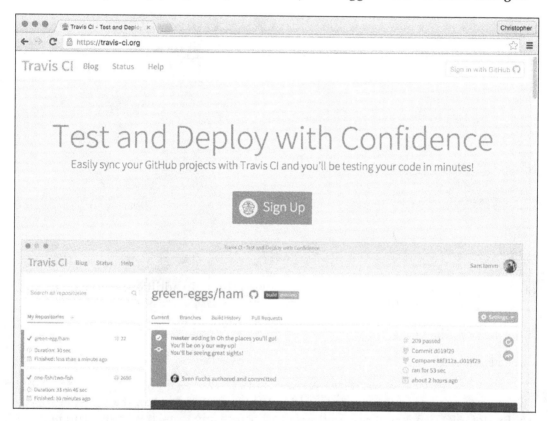

 We will look at how to connect Travis to a GitHub repository, which means we need a GitHub repository already set up. I will not go into detail about how to use GitHub, but you can find an excellent tutorial at `https://guides.github.com/activities/hello-world`.

You can sign in to Travis by logging into your GitHub account and clicking on one of the **Sign in with GitHub** buttons. Hover over your profile and click on **Accounts**:

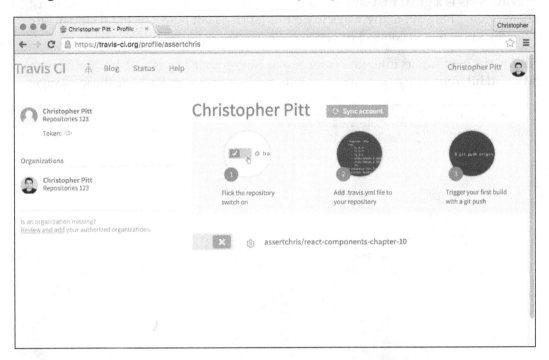

Enable the repositories you would like Travis to check. In addition, you need to create a configuration file called `.travis.yml`:

```
language: node_js

node_js:
  - "5.5"
```

This tells Travis to test this project as a Node.js project and to test it against version 5.5. By default, Travis will run `npm install` before any tests. It will also run `npm test` to run the actual tests. We can enable this command by adding the following to `package.json`:

```
"scripts": {
  "test": "node run.js"
}
```

 If you've put your tests in another file, you'll need to adjust that command to reflect what you type to run your tests. It's nothing more than a common alias.

After you commit code to your repository, Travis should test that code for you.

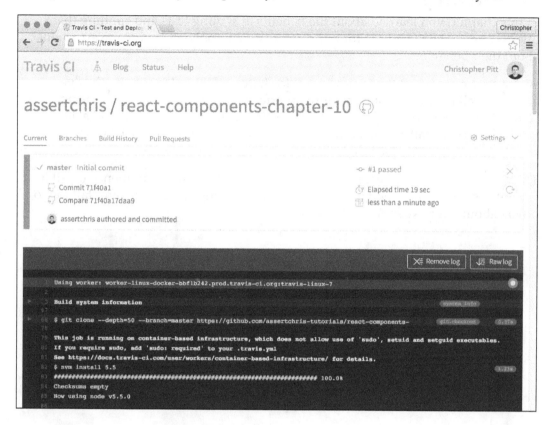

 You can learn more about Travis at `https://docs.travis-ci.com/user/for-beginners`.

End-to-end testing

You may also want to try testing your application as a normal user would. You already do this as you click through the application you're developing to check whether things you just typed work as you expect. Why not automate the process?

There are quite a few tools for this. The one I've enjoyed using is called *Protractor*. It can be a little tricky to set up, but there's an excellent tutorial on the subject at `http://www.joelotter.com/2015/04/18/protractor-reactjs.html`.

Summary

In this chapter, you learned about the benefits of writing tests and running them often. We created a few tests for our classes and components and made assertions about their behavior.

We've now covered all the topics I want to share with you. Hopefully, they've given you all the tools to start creating interfaces with confidence. We've learned so much together; covering topics such as single component designs and states, how components talk to each other (through things such as context), how to structure and decorate the whole system, and even how to test it.

The React community is just beginning, and you can join it and influence it. All it will take is for you to spend a bit of time building things with React and talking to others about your experiences doing so.

Index

A

AdonisJS
  reference link 108
Ajax requests
  communicating through 103, 104
alternatives, for styling React components
  about 59
  CSS modules 59
  React style 59
array tricks
  reference link 28
assertions
  used, for testing 155, 156

B

Babel 6
browser
  code, debugging in 8, 9
  cookie limits, reference link 37
browser history
  using 86-90

C

callbacks
  used, for extending 141-144
code
  debugging, in browser 8, 9
common tasks
  managing 10-12
components
  about 144-148
  lifecycle methods 28-31
  need for 1, 2
  nesting 15-20

rendering, to strings 99, 100
  styles, adding 45-47
cookies
  reference link 37
  validating 36, 37
CSS modules
  about 59
  reference link 59
CSS transitions
  reference link 54
  working with 53-55

D

dangerouslySetInnerHTML
  reference link 106
decorator pattern
  reference link 139
dependency injection
  about 131-133
  importance 137-141
device-independent pixels (dp)
  about 62
  reference link 62

E

edit form
  changing 47-50
  reverting 47-50
  styling 47
elevation
  reference link 62
event emitters
  using 40-42
ExpressJS
  reference link 104

React design patterns
  Flux 116
  Redux 123
React.js Routing
  reference link 91
React Native
  reference link 99
React style
  about 59
  reference link 59
reducers 144-148
Redux
  about 123-127
  benefits 130
  context, using 127-129
  reference link 130
resources
  about 79
  Font Squirrel 79, 80
  Material UI 80
Roboto
  download link 63
router
  using 91-94

S

Sass
  used, for organizing styles 56-59
server backend
  creating 102
server-side applications
  structuring 108, 109
service location 131, 132
service locators 133, 134
shared component actions 20-28
simple server
  creating 101, 102
singleton pattern
  reference link 118
stores 144-148
styles
  adding, to components 45-47
  organizing, Sass used 56-59
SuperAgent
  reference link 104

surfaces
  about 62
  iconography 63
  interactions 63
  motion 63
  typography 63
system icons
  download link 63

T

test-driven development (TDD) 152
testing
  about 151
  connecting, to Travis 159-161
  end-to-end testing 161
  for idempotence 157, 158
  for immutability 157, 158
  used, for designing 152
  used, for documentation 152
  with assertions 155, 156
tests
  functional tests 155
  types 153
  unit tests 153, 154
  used, for discovering regression in
    code 152, 153
Travis
  connecting to 159-161
  reference link 161

U

unit tests 153, 154

W

web sockets
  communicating through 105-108